PAT BROWN, MBA

WrestlingMoney101

Using Wrestling to Teach the Basics of Money

ABRAM 47 BROWN

First published by AbramBrown47 2026

First edition

ISBN: 978-1-967737-63-5

This book was professionally typeset on Reedsy.
Find out more at reedsy.com

Contents

Foreword

Wrestling is honest.

There is no clock to hide behind.

No teammate to cover for you.

No lucky bounce.

When the whistle blows, it is you, your opponent, and the work you put in long before the match ever started.

That honesty is what makes wrestling one of the most demanding sports in the world. It strips away excuses. It exposes preparation. It rewards discipline and punishes shortcuts.

Money works the same way.

There are no style points in financial life. No one cares how confident you feel, how hard you trained, or how much potential you had. Results show up quietly over time. The discipline you practiced or failed to practice eventually reveals itself.

Many athletes leave wrestling believing the hardest part of life is behind them. The conditioning. The weight cuts. The grind. The loneliness. The pressure of stepping onto the mat knowing there is nowhere to hide.

What most do not realize is that the habits forged in wrestling are not meant to end with competition. They are meant to carry forward.

Unfortunately, the structure disappears faster than expected.

In wrestling, everything is controlled for you. Training schedules. Weight classes. Practice times. Accountability. After competition ends, that structure vanishes almost overnight. Suddenly, no one is setting your calendar. No one is checking your discipline. No one is making sure you "make weight" financially.

That is where problems begin.

This book exists because former wrestlers are often *overprepared for pressure* but *underprepared for financial systems.* You know how to suffer. You know how to grind. You know how to compete when it hurts. But no one taught you how to manage income, debt, investing, insurance, and long-term decisions with the same precision you brought to the mat.

That gap is not a failure on your part. It is an education gap.

Wrestling teaches control.

Money requires control.

Wrestling teaches patience.

Money rewards patience.

Wrestling teaches that you cannot skip steps.

Money punishes anyone who tries.

This book is not about getting rich fast. Wrestlers already know better than that. There are no shortcuts that hold up under pressure.

This book is about:

- Making weight financially
- Staying in position instead of forcing moves
- Protecting yourself when the match gets ugly
- Winning one decision at a time over a long season

Just like wrestling, financial success is built through repetition, preparation, and discipline when no one is watching.

Some readers will be current wrestlers. Others will be years removed from competition. That does not matter. The lessons translate either way. The mat may be gone, but the mindset still applies.

You will not find hype in these pages.

You will not find guarantees.

You will not find tricks.

What you will find is a system. A framework. A way to think about money that respects the intelligence, toughness, and discipline wrestling already demanded from you.

If you treat your finances the way you treated your training, your weight management, and your preparation for competition, you will give yourself a real advantage most people never develop.

This is not about nostalgia.

This is about application.

Wrestling trained you for hard things.

Now it is time to apply that training to money.

One decision at a time.

One match at a time.

One season at a time.

Introduction

There is a moment every wrestler remembers.

The handshake is done.

The whistle blows.

And suddenly, everything is quiet.

No teammates on the mat.

No substitutions.

No one to cover for you if you hesitate.

It is just you, your opponent, and the work you put in when no one was watching.

That moment defines wrestling. And in many ways, it defines life after wrestling too.

When competition ends, the structure that guided your days disappears fast. No more mandatory practices. No weight checks. No coaches setting the schedule. No clear opponent standing across from you. Instead, you are handed responsibility for everything at once.

Income.

Bills.

Debt.

Savings.

Investing.

Insurance.

Long-term decisions that carry consequences you may not see for years.

There is no whistle to reset the situation. No coach calling timeout. No one stepping in to fix a mistake before it costs you.

You are on your own.

This is where many former wrestlers feel disoriented. Not because they lack discipline, but because the environment changed completely. Wrestling trained you to respond to structure. Life after wrestling requires you to create it.

That transition is harder than most people admit.

In wrestling, the path is clear. Make weight. Train hard. Execute. Adjust. Repeat. Financial life does not come with that clarity. Decisions arrive without warning. Consequences show up quietly. Feedback is delayed. You can be doing something wrong for years before it becomes obvious.

That delay is dangerous.

Many athletes assume financial problems come from laziness or irresponsibility. That is rarely true. More often, the issue is a lack of systems. Wrestlers are exceptional at following systems. Few are taught how to build their own.

Money exposes that gap.

You might earn more than your peers and still feel behind.

You might work harder and still feel stressed.

You might make good money decisions occasionally but lack consistency.

That inconsistency is not a character flaw. It is a structure problem.

Wrestling teaches you to control what you can control. Your conditioning. Your preparation. Your effort. Financial success works the same way. You cannot control markets, employers, or unexpected events. You can control habits, decisions, and discipline.

This book is designed to help you rebuild structure after the whistle blows.

It uses wrestling because wrestling already taught you the hardest lessons. Discipline. Sacrifice. Patience. Accountability. You learned how to suffer now so you could perform later. Money rewards that exact mindset.

But money also punishes freelancing.

Cutting corners.

Chasing quick wins.

Ignoring fundamentals.

Assuming strength alone is enough.

In wrestling, those mistakes get exposed immediately. In money, they get exposed years later. That delay makes them more expensive.

This book does not assume you want complexity. Wrestlers value clarity. Simple plans executed consistently beat complicated plans executed poorly. The goal here is not perfection. It is control.

Control of cash flow.

Control of risk.

Control of decisions under pressure.

Just like on the mat, control keeps you in position. It allows you to defend when necessary and attack when the opportunity is real.

Life after wrestling is not a single match. It is a long season. There will be good stretches and bad ones. Injuries, setbacks, and surprises will happen. The goal is not to dominate every moment. The goal is to stay in the match.

You already know how to do that.

You did it in the room.

You did it during weight cuts.

You did it when no one was watching.

Now it is time to apply that discipline somewhere new.

When the whistle blows in life, you are on your own.

This book is here to help you wrestle well anyway.

About This Book

Wrestling is one of the purest sports there is.

No clock to hide behind.

No teammates to bail you out.

No shortcuts that last very long.

Every match is a direct reflection of preparation, discipline, and control.

Money works the same way.

This book exists because the lessons wrestlers learn on the mat translate almost perfectly to financial life, yet no one ever connects the two. Wrestlers graduate with elite discipline, pain tolerance, and work ethic, but are sent into adulthood without a financial framework that matches those traits.

The result is frustration.

Wrestlers are used to clear rules.

Clear weight classes.

Clear scoring.

Clear consequences.

Money rarely feels that clear. The feedback is delayed. The rules are confusing. Mistakes compound quietly. You can be doing things wrong for years before the damage becomes obvious.

That gap is not your fault.

This book is built to close it using a language you already understand.

Wrestling Is a Game of Control, Not Flash

The best wrestlers are not always the most explosive. They are the most controlled.

They manage position.

They understand leverage.

They stay patient.

They win small exchanges over and over again.

Championships are built on consistency, not desperation.

Financial success follows the same pattern.

Most money problems come from trying to force outcomes. Chasing quick wins. Ignoring fundamentals. Cutting weight the wrong way. Taking risks that feel aggressive but leave you exposed.

Wrestling teaches you that shortcuts cost you later. So does money.

This book treats finances the way wrestling treats matches. You win by staying in position, protecting yourself, and choosing the right moments to attack. Not by swinging wildly and hoping something works.

Discipline Is Transferable, Systems Are Not

Wrestling gave you discipline. It did not give you a financial system.

You learned how to show up tired.

How to train without applause.

How to control emotions under pressure.

Those traits matter more in money than raw intelligence ever will. But discipline without structure eventually breaks down. In wrestling, coaches provided that structure. After wrestling, you are expected to create it yourself.

That is where most former wrestlers struggle.

Not because they are undisciplined, but because no one showed them how to build systems for adult life. Budgeting, saving, investing, insurance, and planning require structure the same way training cycles do.

This book shows you how to build that structure using wrestling logic.

Making Weight Is a Financial Skill

Wrestlers understand limits.

You cannot ignore weight classes.

You cannot eat whatever you want and expect performance.

You cannot outwork bad habits forever.

Money has limits too.

Income is not infinite.

Energy is not infinite.

Time is not infinite.

Budgeting, saving, and managing debt are the financial equivalent of making weight responsibly. Done correctly, they give you freedom. Done poorly, they drain performance and shorten careers.

This book reframes financial discipline as performance management, not deprivation.

Position Wins Matches, Protection Wins Financial Careers

In wrestling, position matters more than effort alone.

You can work incredibly hard from a bad position and still lose. Smart wrestlers protect themselves first. They defend before they attack. They avoid getting pinned early.

Financial protection works the same way.

Emergency funds.

Insurance.

Risk management.

These are not signs of fear. They are signs of intelligence. You cannot build a financial life if one unexpected event can pin you immediately.

This book emphasizes defense first because defense keeps you in the match.

One Match at a Time, One Decision at a Time

Wrestlers do not win seasons in one match. They win them by stacking disciplined performances over time.

Money rewards the same approach.

You do not need perfect decisions.

You need repeatable ones.

You do not need genius.

You need consistency.

This book is written one chapter at a time, just like training cycles and matches. Each section builds on the last. Nothing is designed to overwhelm you. Everything is designed to be executable.

Why This Book Is Different

This is not a finance textbook.

This is not motivational fluff.

This is not theory.

This is a playbook written for wrestlers who respect hard truths, structure, and accountability.

Wrestling already taught you how to win difficult battles.

This book teaches you how to apply that same mindset to money, one match at a time.

Foolish Assumptions

Every coach makes assumptions.

Not because they are careless, but because assumptions shape how a plan is built. A conditioning program assumes you will show up. A practice plan assumes you will listen, compete, and hold yourself accountable. Wrestling demands honesty. If the assumptions are wrong, the system fails quickly.

This book makes a few assumptions about you.

They may feel uncomfortable at times. That is intentional. Growth in wrestling never came from comfort, and neither does financial progress.

This Book Assumes You Know How to Work Hard

Wrestling is not a sport you stumble into.

If you have competed, you already understand effort. You know what it means to train when tired, to cut weight responsibly or irresponsibly, to grind through long practices, and to compete under pressure without excuses.

This book assumes effort is not your problem.

If money has been difficult, it is not because you lack discipline. It is because no one gave you a financial structure that matched the discipline you already have.

You do not need motivation.

You need a system.

This Book Assumes You Respect Accountability

Wrestlers live in accountability.

The scale does not lie.

The scoreboard does not lie.

The film does not lie.

You cannot talk your way out of a loss. You cannot blame teammates. You cannot hide from results.

This book assumes you are willing to look honestly at your financial situation. Income. Spending. Debt. Habits. Mistakes.

If you are looking for validation, this is not the right book.

If you are looking for progress, you are in the right place.

This Book Assumes You Can Handle Delayed Feedback

One of the hardest parts of money is that feedback is slow.

You can make a bad decision today and not feel the consequences for years. You can also do the right thing for a long time before seeing visible progress.

Wrestling prepared you for that.

You trained for months for matches that lasted minutes. You trusted the process even when results were not immediate. This book assumes you can apply that same patience to money.

Financial success is not about one decision. It is about stacking disciplined behavior over time.

This Book Assumes You Want Control, Not Shortcuts

Wrestling exposes shortcuts immediately.

Bad weight cuts show up in the third period.

Poor conditioning shows up late in matches.

Skipping fundamentals shows up against better opponents.

Money works the same way.

This book assumes you are not looking for hacks, tricks, or "one weird move" that changes everything. Those approaches fail under pressure.

Instead, this book assumes you want control.

Control of cash flow.

Control of risk.

Control of decisions.

Control beats flash. Always has.

This Book Assumes You Are Willing to Be a Beginner Again

This assumption is the hardest.

You may have been elite in your sport. Respected. Confident. Certain. Money may not feel that way.

This book assumes you are willing to learn without ego.

Wrestlers who last are coachable. They listen. They adjust. They accept feedback. Financial growth requires the same humility.

You do not need to know everything.

You need to be willing to learn.

This Book Assumes You Want a Long Career, Not a Highlight Reel

Wrestling teaches you that longevity matters.

You do not win championships by burning out early. You win by staying healthy, managing energy, and making smart decisions season after season.

This book assumes you want the same outcome financially.

Not quick wins.

Not status.

Not comparison.

But stability.

Freedom.

Options.

A Final Reality Check

If these assumptions bother you, that is not a problem. Wrestling always exposed weak spots before growth happened.

This book assumes you are capable of more than you think.

It assumes you are disciplined enough to execute.

It assumes you want a financial life that holds up under pressure.

Those are not foolish assumptions.

They are earned.

How This Playbook Is Organized

Wrestling does not reward chaos.

Every practice has a purpose. Every drill builds toward a position. Every match is broken into periods, situations, and decisions. You do not just "go wrestle" and hope it works out. You prepare in layers, mastering fundamentals before adding complexity.

This book is organized the same way.

It is not meant to be read like a textbook. It is meant to be used like a training plan. You can read it straight through, or you can jump to the chapter that matches where you are right now. Either way, the structure matters, because each section builds on the one before it.

Front Matter: Setting the Mental Frame

Before you step on the mat, your mindset matters.

The **Foreword**, **Introduction**, and early sections exist to reset expectations. Life after wrestling feels different because the structure is gone. The whistle blows, and suddenly you are responsible for decisions that used to be handled for you.

These opening sections explain why money feels overwhelming, why that is normal, and why your wrestling background is actually an advantage if you use it correctly. This is about getting your head right before you start making decisions.

Part I: Weight Class and Fundamentals

You cannot win if you do not make weight.

Part I is about fundamentals. Cash flow. Budgeting. Banking. Credit. These are the basics that determine whether you are even eligible to compete financially.

Just like wrestling, if you ignore fundamentals, everything else breaks down. You cannot out-technique bad conditioning, and you cannot out-invest poor cash flow.

This section is intentionally practical. It focuses on awareness, discipline, and control. Nothing flashy. Nothing complicated. Just the habits that keep you in position.

If money has ever felt chaotic, this is where order begins.

Part II: Defense, Positioning, and Protection

Position wins matches.

Once fundamentals are in place, you learn how to protect yourself. Risk awareness. Insurance. Defensive assets like bonds and diversified funds. This section is about avoiding unnecessary exposure.

In wrestling, good defense does not mean passive wrestling. It means staying in position so your opponent cannot capitalize on mistakes. Financial defense works the same way.

This section teaches you how to recognize risk, protect what you earn, and stay composed when pressure shows up. It is about staying available for the long season.

Part III: Getting on Base (Investing Fundamentals)

You do not need a pin every match to win tournaments.

Part III introduces investing fundamentals using the same logic wrestlers already understand. Base hits matter. Reps matter. Consistency matters.

You will learn how markets work, how compounding actually builds over time, and why chasing highlights usually leads to losses. This section focuses on ownership, patience, and execution, not speculation.

This is where long-term growth begins, but only after the foundation is solid.

Part IV: Match Management and Adjustments

Championships are not won by ego. They are won by adjustments.

This section is about managing what you have built. Asset allocation. Buying and holding. Rebalancing. Mental discipline.

Just like between periods, this is where you check the score, adjust strategy, and avoid overreacting. Many people lose financially not because they make bad decisions, but because they change plans too often.

This part teaches you how to stay disciplined, review intelligently, and trust the process.

Part V: Life After the Mat

Eventually, the season ends.

This section addresses the realities of long-term life decisions. Taxes. Retirement. Housing. Career transitions. Estate planning. Family conversations.

Wrestling may end, but responsibility does not. This section helps you apply the same preparation mindset to life stages that arrive whether you are ready or not.

Part VI: Winning the Long Season

The final section ties everything together.

It focuses on advisors, avoiding scams, recognizing bad advice, and building rules that protect you over decades, not months. This is about staying in the game long after the uniform comes off.

How to Use This Book

You do not need to read every word at once.

Read it like you trained:

- One rep at a time
- One concept at a time
- One adjustment at a time

Come back to it when life changes. Revisit chapters when decisions get bigger. Use it as a reference, not a finish line.

This playbook is not about perfection.

It is about control, discipline, and staying in position.

Just like wrestling.

About Pat Brown

Pat Brown understands discipline before he ever talked about money.

He learned it in the locker room.

Pat played college football at the University of Kansas from 1994 to 1999 and was named team captain for the 1999 season. Those years were defined by early mornings, accountability, physical discomfort, and the kind of pressure that reveals who you really are. Nobody in that environment gets a free pass. You earn your role. You do your job. You are responsible not just for yourself, but for the people next to you.

That experience shaped how Pat sees everything that came after football.

When the uniform came off, the structure disappeared. There was no strength coach setting the schedule. No position coach reviewing film. No one checking effort. Like many former athletes, Pat had to rebuild structure on his own. What he carried with him from football was the understanding that success is not accidental. It is built through preparation, discipline, and consistency, especially when no one is watching.

After football, Pat transitioned into financial services and built a career as a financial advisor and wealth manager. He works with individuals, families, business owners, and athletes navigating increasingly complex financial lives. Over time, he saw the same patterns repeat. Smart, driven people making avoidable mistakes not because they lacked intelligence, but because they lacked a system.

Pat pursued advanced education to deepen his ability to help people build those systems. He earned an MBA and industry designations including ChFC®, RICP®, and CAP®. His background blends academic training with real-world experience in financial planning, retirement income strategies, tax planning, and philanthropy. But credentials were never the point.

Practical application was.

As the college sports landscape changed with the introduction of Name, Image, and Likeness opportunities, a familiar problem became impossible to ignore. Student athletes were gaining access to income, contracts, and endorsements without the financial knowledge required to manage taxes, cash flow, business structures, and long-term consequences.

The same discipline athletes were expected to show on the mat or field was not being applied to money, simply because no one had taught them how.

That gap became the catalyst for Pat's work in athlete financial education.

He began focusing on building resources that met athletes where they are. Not academic theory. Not complicated jargon. Real-world guidance using the language athletes already understand. Preparation. Reps. Film study. Adjustments. Discipline under pressure.

Pat has since become a recognized voice in athlete financial education and has been interviewed by national publications and platforms including *Financial Planning*, *Yahoo*, and *ESPN Andscape*. In those conversations, he consistently highlights the same issue. Opportunity without education creates risk. Financial literacy has to arrive before money shows up, not after mistakes are made.

That belief led Pat to author a growing series of athlete-focused books designed to translate sports culture into financial decision-making. His NIL-related titles include *Financial Literacy for NIL*, *Financial Literacy for NIL for Parents of Student Athletes*, *Financial Literacy for NIL for High School Students*, and *Financial Literacy for NIL for International Student Athletes*. Each book is written to be clear, accessible, and grounded in real-life scenarios athletes and families actually face.

He also created a broad collection of sport-specific financial education titles, including *Football Money 101*, *Baseball Money 101*, *Basketball Money 101*, *Cheer Money 101*, *Dance Money 101*, *Gymnastics Money 101*, *Hockey Money 101*, *Lacrosse Money 101*, *Rowing Money 101*, *Soccer Money 101*, *Softball Money 101*, *Tennis Money 101*, *Track Money 101*, *Volleyball Money 101*, and *Wrestling Money 101*. Each book respects the culture of the sport and uses it as the foundation for teaching money skills athletes can carry into life after competition.

To extend this mission beyond books, Pat founded **Former Student Athlete**, a platform created to support athletes navigating life after sports. The platform focuses on financial literacy, career transitions, health, identity, and long-term success once the uniform comes off. That work continues at:

- www.formerstudentathlete.com
- www.financialliteracyfornil.com
- www.financialliteracyforstudentathletes.com

Pat is easy to find through a Google search, on LinkedIn, or on Twitter, where he regularly shares insights on athletes, money, and life after sports. If you would like to connect specifically about *Wrestling Money 101,* Pat believes the conversation should be practical, honest, and focused on helping athletes stay in control long after competition ends.

At his core, Pat's work is driven by a belief shaped by both football and finance.

Athletes deserve a better playbook for life after sports.

And financial education should arrive before opportunity turns into regret.

Part I: Weight Class and Fundamentals

You cannot win if you do not make weight.

Every wrestler understands this truth before the first whistle ever blows.

You can be strong. You can be skilled. You can have the best technique in the room. None of it matters if you miss weight. If you cannot step on the scale and qualify to compete, the match is over before it starts. No excuses. No appeals. No "almost."

Money works the same way.

Before strategy, before investing, before long-term planning, you have to be eligible to compete financially. That eligibility comes from fundamentals. Cash flow. Spending control. Basic systems. Discipline. These are not exciting topics, but they are non-negotiable.

This part of the book is your weight cut.

Not the dangerous, reckless kind. The disciplined, controlled kind that sets you up to perform when it counts.

Why Fundamentals Decide Everything

In wrestling, fundamentals show up everywhere. Stance. Balance. Hand fighting. Conditioning. You drill them every day, not because they are flashy, but because they hold up under pressure. When fatigue sets in and emotions spike, fundamentals are what remain.

Financial fundamentals work the same way.

When income changes.

When expenses spike.

When life hits unexpectedly.

When opportunities appear suddenly.

If your foundation is weak, stress exposes it immediately. Missed payments. Panic decisions. Debt accumulation. Forced choices. If your foundation is solid, you stay composed. You adjust. You keep control of the match.

You cannot skip this phase and expect good outcomes later.

Making Weight Financially

Making weight financially means a few simple things:

You know what comes in.

You know what goes out.

You can cover basic expenses without panic.

You have some margin for mistakes.

You are not relying on credit to survive.

That is it.

Not wealth. Not freedom. Not dominance. Eligibility.

Just like wrestling, this is not about perfection. It is about consistency and honesty. Stepping on the scale does not care about effort. It reflects reality. Your bank account does the same.

This section forces you to look at reality without judgment, because avoiding the scale does not change the number.

Discipline Over Flash

Wrestling teaches a lesson that transfers directly to money.

Discipline beats flash.

A disciplined wrestler with average talent beats a talented wrestler with poor habits more often than people like to admit. Weight management. Conditioning. Recovery. Mental toughness. These quiet habits decide outcomes.

Financially, discipline looks like:

Saving before spending.

Tracking instead of guessing.

Planning instead of reacting.

Staying patient instead of forcing results.

Flashy financial moves get attention. Fundamentals build longevity.

Control Before Aggression

In wrestling, you earn the right to attack by controlling position. You do not shoot wildly from bad angles and hope it works. You create openings by doing the small things right.

Money works the same way.

Before investing aggressively.

Before taking on leverage.

Before chasing growth.

You need control.

Control of cash flow.

Control of spending.

Control of habits.

Control of emotions.

Aggression without control leads to exposure. Exposure leads to mistakes. Mistakes end seasons.

What This Section Will Do for You

Part I is not about growth yet. It is about stability.

It will help you:

- Understand why money feels overwhelming after wrestling
- See your financial situation clearly and honestly
- Build simple systems that reduce stress
- Replace extreme behavior with sustainable habits

This is where you rebuild structure after the sport is gone.

Nobody is setting your schedule anymore.

Nobody is checking your weight.

Nobody is enforcing discipline.

That responsibility is now yours.

The good news is this: wrestlers are uniquely prepared for this phase. You already know how to do hard things consistently. You already understand sacrifice for long-term payoff. You already know that the scale does not lie.

This section simply teaches you how to apply that mindset to money.

Make weight first.

Everything else comes after.

Chapter 1: Why Money Feels Overwhelming After Wrestling

Every wrestler remembers the first real match that mattered.

The gym feels louder. The mat feels smaller. The clock moves differently. Moves you drilled a thousand times suddenly feel rushed. It is not because you were unprepared. It is because pressure changes how information shows up.

Money feels overwhelming for the same reason.

Most wrestlers do not struggle financially because they are careless, lazy, or irresponsible. They struggle because they are asked to manage real financial decisions without structure, without coaching, and without reps. One day, wrestling controls nearly every variable in your life. Training time. Meals. Weight. Travel. Competition schedule. Accountability. Then the whistle blows for the last time, and suddenly you are on your own.

No weigh-ins.

No coaches checking habits.

No daily structure.

Just decisions.

That is why money feels heavy after wrestling.

Why Financial Literacy Is Rarely Taught to Athletes

Wrestling is built on control and simplicity. The sport strips life down to basics. Train. Eat. Recover. Compete. Repeat. That environment creates discipline, but it also removes the need to think about many everyday systems.

Financial literacy usually falls through the cracks for a few reasons.

First, everyone assumes someone else will teach it. Schools assume families handle it. Families assume athletes will learn it later. Coaches focus on performance, not paychecks. By the time income, scholarships, stipends, or real jobs appear, education is already late.

Second, wrestling culture rewards toughness, not questions. You are taught to push through discomfort, not slow down and ask for explanations. Money confusion often feels like weakness, so athletes stay quiet.

Third, structure hides consequences. In wrestling, mistakes get corrected immediately. Miss weight, and the consequences are instant. Miss a financial decision, and the damage may not show up for years. That delay makes learning harder.

Wrestling prepares you to suffer for progress. It does not prepare you to manage cash flow, credit, or long-term planning without guidance.

That gap is not your fault. But it becomes your responsibility.

Money Myths Passed Through Locker Rooms and Gyms

Every wrestling room has money talk.

Someone knows a former teammate who made fast money investing. Someone else says debt is always bad. Another claims saving is pointless if you are not rich yet. The most confident voice often sounds the smartest, even when it is wrong.

Common myths sound like this:

"If you are not investing, you are falling behind."

"Being aggressive is the only way to win."

"Saving is for people who do not make much."

"Debt is either evil or free money."

These ideas spread because they are simple and emotional. Wrestling rooms thrive on emotion. Unfortunately, money does not.

You would never overhaul your entire wrestling style because one guy said it worked for him. Financial myths deserve the same skepticism. Context matters. Timing matters. Individual situations matter.

Blindly following locker room advice is like copying someone else's weight cut without knowing their body. It works until it does not.

Saving vs Investing vs Gambling

This is where most confusion begins.

Saving, investing, and gambling are not the same thing, even though people often lump them together.

Saving is about protection. It is money you can access quickly. Emergency funds. Short-term needs. Stability. Saving keeps you eligible to compete financially. It prevents panic when something unexpected happens.

Investing is about ownership and growth over time. It requires patience and discipline. Ups and downs are normal. Progress comes from staying consistent, not reacting emotionally.

Gambling is chasing outcomes without protection. No margin. No system. Emotion-driven decisions based on excitement, fear, or ego.

In wrestling terms, saving is conditioning. It is not glamorous, but without it, you gas out early. Investing is positional control. You build advantages slowly and deliberately. Gambling is throwing a desperate move from a bad position and hoping it works.

Many wrestlers skip saving because it feels slow. They jump straight into investing or speculation. That is like skipping conditioning and expecting to win deep into the third period. It works occasionally. Long term, it fails.

Why Discipline Beats Flashy Moves

Wrestling punishes flashy mistakes.

A reckless throw can end a match instantly. A sloppy shot can put you on your back. The best wrestlers win by controlling position, not by chasing highlights.

Money works the same way.

Flashy financial moves get attention. Big wins get talked about. Quiet discipline rarely does. But discipline is what holds up under pressure.

Discipline looks like:

Saving consistently, even when it feels boring

Spending intentionally, not emotionally

Building systems instead of relying on willpower

Staying patient when progress feels slow

Just like wrestling, money rewards the athlete who can do the same simple things over and over without getting bored.

The Loss of Structure After Wrestling

One of the hardest transitions after wrestling is the loss of enforced structure.

No one sets your schedule.

No one monitors your habits.

No one checks your preparation.

That freedom sounds appealing until you realize structure was doing more work than you thought. Without it, small decisions pile up. Skipped habits become patterns. Financial mistakes compound quietly.

This is where many former wrestlers struggle. Not because they lack discipline, but because discipline was externally enforced for so long. Money requires internal discipline.

The good news is that wrestling already taught you how to build discipline. You just have to apply it without a whistle.

Coach's Perspective

If your coach were talking about money, the message would be familiar.

Make weight every day.

Control what you can control.

Do not chase flashy moves.

Win the position before you attack.

Trust the process.

Money does not need heroics. It needs fundamentals executed consistently. Coaches never stop teaching fundamentals because fundamentals win under pressure.

Game Situations and Decision Points

You get your first steady paycheck. Do you save first, or spend and hope there is something left?

You hear about a fast opportunity. Do you jump in because others are doing it, or ask if it fits your situation?

You have no emergency fund. Do you ignore the risk and hope nothing happens, or start building protection now?

Just like wrestling, these are match-deciding moments. The decision matters more than the emotion.

Common Wrestler Mistakes and Financial Parallels

Wrestlers cut corners on weight.

Financially, that looks like ignoring savings.

Wrestlers chase big moves from bad positions.

Financially, that looks like chasing fast money.

Wrestlers underestimate recovery.

Financially, that leads to burnout and debt.

The same habits that lose matches lose money.

Winning the Long Game

Wrestling careers are short. Financial lives are long.

You do not need to win every day. You need to stay eligible to compete. Discipline creates options. Options reduce stress. Reduced stress leads to better decisions.

Money becomes less overwhelming when you stop trying to dominate it and start managing it one match at a time.

Athlete Takeaways

- Make weight first. Eligibility matters more than flash.
- Saving protects you. Investing grows you. Gambling guesses.
- Locker room money advice is not a game plan.
- Discipline beats flashy moves over time.
- Control position before you attack.

Chapter 2: Step on the Scale

Your Financial Snapshot

Every wrestler knows this moment.

You step on the scale. No excuses. No explanations. No emotion. The number either makes weight or it does not. It does not care how hard training was. It does not care how disciplined you felt. It shows reality.

Money has a scale too.

Most people avoid it. Not because they are reckless, but because no one taught them how to read it without judgment. Bank balances feel scattered. Bills arrive at different times. Spending happens automatically. Instead of stepping on the scale, people rely on how they feel.

That is how small problems turn into big ones.

Before you adjust your training, before you cut weight, before you change strategy, you check the number. Financial progress starts the same way. You need a snapshot of where you actually are.

Income, Expenses, and Cash Flow

Cash flow is the heartbeat of your finances.

Income is what comes in. Paychecks. Bonuses. Side work. NIL income for some athletes.

Expenses are what go out. Rent. Food. Transportation. Subscriptions.

Lifestyle spending.

Cash flow is the difference between the two.

In wrestling terms, income is calories in. Expenses are calories burned. Cash flow determines whether you maintain weight, gain, or slowly drift out of your class.

A lot of former wrestlers focus only on income. More money feels like progress. Just like eating more feels powerful when training hard. But if output rises at the same rate, nothing changes. Worse, you may slowly lose control.

Positive cash flow gives you options. Negative cash flow creates pressure. Pressure leads to panic decisions, just like a bad weight cut.

You do not need complex spreadsheets. You need awareness. Know what comes in. Know what goes out. Everything else builds from there.

Assets, Liabilities, and Net Worth

This is where the snapshot deepens.

Assets are things you own that have value.

Cash. Investments. Property. Businesses.

Liabilities are what you owe.

Credit cards. Student loans. Car loans. Mortgages.

Net worth is the difference.

In wrestling terms, assets are your strengths. Conditioning. Technique. Experience. Liabilities are vulnerabilities. Injuries. Poor positioning. Bad habits. Net worth is your overall match position.

One strong asset does not cancel out multiple weaknesses. One good paycheck does not erase high debt or poor habits. You have to look at the full picture.

Many athletes confuse income with wealth. Income is what you earn this month. Net worth is what you keep and build over time. Wrestlers understand this intuitively. A single good match does not define a season. Consistent positioning does.

Fixed vs Variable Expenses

Not all expenses are created equal.

Fixed expenses are mostly stable. Rent. Insurance. Loan payments.

Variable expenses change month to month. Food. Travel. Entertainment. Convenience spending.

Fixed expenses are like your base stance. They set your structure. Variable expenses are where adjustments happen.

Most people try to cut big fixed costs first, which is often difficult and stressful. The real leverage is usually in variable spending you barely notice. Small purchases. Repeated habits. Convenience decisions made under fatigue.

In wrestling terms, this is poor hand fighting. One slip does not end the match. Repeated mistakes do.

Little leaks add up over a season.

Film Review: Where Your Money Actually Goes

This is the hardest part, and the most important.

Pull your bank statements. Pull your credit card statements. Look at them honestly. No judgment. No shame. Just facts.

Film review is not punishment. It is improvement.

You may notice subscriptions you forgot about. Spending patterns that do not align with your goals. Habits driven by convenience, not intention. None of this makes you weak. It makes you human.

Avoiding the film does not make mistakes disappear. It guarantees they repeat.

Wrestlers who skip film keep getting hit with the same move. Financially, the same rule applies.

Why Awareness Changes Everything

Once you see the numbers, something shifts.

You stop guessing.

You stop assuming.

You stop blaming external factors.

You start making adjustments.

Awareness gives you control. Control reduces stress. Reduced stress improves decision-making. This is how discipline compounds.

Most financial problems are not emergencies. They are slow drifts. The scale catches drift early, before it becomes a crisis.

Coach's Perspective

A coach would not let you guess your weight.

The scale does not lie.

The film does not lie.

Details matter.

If you do not look at it, you cannot fix it.

Avoiding the snapshot does not protect you. It exposes you.

Match Situations and Decision Points

You feel like you are doing fine, but your balance never grows. Do you blame income, or check spending?

You get a raise. Do you increase lifestyle immediately, or improve cash flow first?

You have debt but no clear list of what you owe. Do you ignore it, or write it all down and face it?

Just like wrestling, progress starts with honest evaluation.

Common Wrestler Mistakes and Financial Parallels

Wrestlers avoid the scale until the last minute.

Financially, that looks like avoiding statements.

Wrestlers rely on feel instead of data.

Financially, that means guessing instead of tracking.

Wrestlers celebrate one good match.

Financially, that means one paycheck hiding bad habits.

The same avoidance patterns repeat.

Winning the Long Match

Great wrestlers check weight early and often. Not to punish themselves, but to stay eligible to compete. Money works the same way.

Your financial snapshot is not about judgment. It is about awareness. Awareness keeps you in control. Control keeps you calm. Calm keeps you disciplined.

This is how you stop getting pinned by problems you never saw coming.

Athlete Takeaways

- Step on the scale. Numbers beat feelings.
- Cash flow decides whether you are in control or under pressure.
- Assets build strength. Liabilities create exposure.
- Fixed costs set structure. Variable costs decide outcomes.
- Watch the film. Awareness is how you win the next match.

Chapter 3: Cutting Weight the Right Way

Budgeting and Saving

Every wrestler has seen it done the wrong way.

Last-minute cuts. Trash bags. Starving. Dehydrating. Panic. You might make weight, but you are weak, foggy, and exposed the moment the whistle blows. You survived the scale, but you did not prepare to compete.

Money works the same way.

A lot of people treat budgeting and saving like crash weight cuts. They wait until something goes wrong. Credit card balances spike. Accounts run low. Stress hits. Then they scramble. Cut everything. Overcorrect. Feel miserable. Quit.

That is not discipline. That is damage control.

Winning financially requires cutting weight the right way. Slow. Intentional. Repeatable. Sustainable.

Budgeting Systems That Actually Work

A budget is not punishment.

It is not restriction.

It is not saying no to everything.

It is not tracking every dollar with anxiety.

A budget is a training plan.

In wrestling terms, budgeting is knowing your weight class and how to stay there all season. You are not guessing day to day. You know what fuels you. You know what drains you. You know the limits.

The best budgeting systems share a few traits:

- **Simple**: If it is complicated, you will abandon it under stress.
- **Realistic**: If it ignores real life, it will fail.
- **Repeatable**: If you cannot run it every month, it does not work.

At its core, a budget answers three questions:

1. How much comes in?
2. What has to go out?
3. What is left to deploy intentionally?

That is it.

Everything else is detail. Just like wrestling. The fundamentals matter more than flashy technique.

You do not need a perfect plan. You need one you can execute when tired, busy, and distracted.

Why Most Budgets Fail Wrestlers

Most budgets fail because they are built on willpower instead of systems.

Wrestlers understand this immediately. You do not rely on motivation to make weight. You rely on structure. Meals. Timing. Hydration. Conditioning. Reps.

Financially, relying on motivation sounds like this:

"I'll save what's left over."

"I'll be better next month."

"I just need more income."

That is the equivalent of saying you will cut weight later. It rarely works.

Discipline beats motivation. Systems beat intentions.

Automating Savings Like Daily Conditioning

Conditioning is not optional.

You do it whether you feel like it or not. It is built into practice. Built into the week. Built into the season. You do not debate it every day.

Saving should work the same way.

If you wait to save what is left at the end of the month, you will usually save nothing. Life expands. Convenience wins. Fatigue makes decisions sloppy.

Automation fixes this.

- Direct deposit into savings
- Automatic transfers after payday
- Scheduled contributions to long-term accounts

In wrestling terms, this is daily conditioning. You may not see the results immediately, but the edge compounds. Automation removes emotion, and emotion is where financial mistakes live.

You are not depending on discipline in the moment. You are building discipline into the system.

Emergency Funds as Injury Insurance

Every wrestler understands injury risk.

You do not plan to get hurt. You prepare anyway. Trainers. Rehab plans. Backup lineups. Recovery protocols. Injuries are part of the sport.

An emergency fund is financial injury insurance.

It is cash set aside for the unexpected. Car repairs. Medical bills. Job changes. Delayed income. Life.

Without an emergency fund, every surprise becomes a crisis. You reach for credit. You panic. You abandon the plan. That is how bad habits form.

With an emergency fund, you stay composed. You absorb the hit and keep wrestling.

That composure is everything.

An emergency fund does not make you rich. It keeps you from getting pinned by one bad moment.

How Much Is Enough?

There is no magic number.

A common target is three to six months of essential expenses. The exact amount depends on:

- Income stability
- Career stage
- Health
- Family responsibilities

In wrestling terms, this is conditioning for your weight class. A heavyweight and a lightweight do not train the same way. The goal is readiness, not comparison.

Balancing Lifestyle With Long-Term Goals

This is where many former wrestlers struggle.

You trained hard. You sacrificed. You cut weight. You lived disciplined for years. When competition ends, it is natural to want freedom.

That desire is valid.

The mistake is turning short-term comfort into long-term constraint.

Wrestling teaches delayed gratification. You suffer now to perform later. Money requires the same mindset.

You do not have to live miserably. You do have to be intentional.

- Spend on what actually matters to you
- Cut what does not
- Protect future options

Lifestyle choices should support your life, not quietly limit it.

The Difference Between Control and Deprivation

Cutting weight the right way never feels like punishment.

It feels controlled.

You are fueled. You are sharp. You are confident stepping on the scale. Budgeting and saving should feel the same way.

If your system makes you miserable, it will not last. If it gives you control, it will compound.

Coach's Perspective

A coach would be blunt.

Make weight the right way.

Do not cheat the process.

Discipline is freedom.

Control the little things.

Budgets and savings are boring for the same reason conditioning is boring. They work.

Match Situations and Decision Points

You get paid. Do you save first, or hope there is something left?

You want to upgrade your lifestyle. Do you check the plan, or ignore it?

An unexpected expense hits. Do you stay calm with cash, or reach for credit?

These are match-by-match decisions. Over time, they decide seasons.

Common Wrestler Mistakes and Financial Parallels

Wrestlers crash cut weight.

Financially, that looks like panic budgeting.

Wrestlers skip conditioning.

Financially, that looks like skipping savings.

Wrestlers reward hard work with shortcuts.

Financially, that shows up as lifestyle creep.

The habits are the same. The consequences just take longer to show up.

Winning the Long Match

Championship wrestlers make weight all season, not just once. They control the process so performance is available when it matters.

Budgeting and saving give you the same edge. Control creates calm. Calm creates discipline. Discipline creates options.

This is how you stay competitive long after the mat is gone.

Athlete Takeaways

- A budget is a training plan, not a punishment.
- Automate savings the way you automate conditioning.
- Emergency funds keep you from getting pinned by surprises.
- Lifestyle choices today affect flexibility tomorrow.
- Cut weight with control, not panic.

Chapter 4: Borrowed Leverage

Credit and Debt

Every wrestler understands leverage.

Used correctly, leverage lets a smaller, less powerful athlete control someone stronger. Position, timing, pressure, and angles matter more than brute force. Used poorly, leverage backfires fast. You reach. You overextend. You get reversed. You get pinned.

Credit and debt work the same way.

Borrowed money is leverage. It can help you move forward when applied intentionally. It can also put you on your back early in the match if you lose control. The problem is not debt itself. The problem is misunderstanding how it works and when it should be used.

Wrestlers do not fear leverage. They respect it. That is the mindset you need with credit and debt.

How Credit Scores and Reports Work

Your credit score is not a judgment of who you are as a person.

It is a record of how you handle borrowed leverage.

Think of your credit report as film. Every loan, every card, every payment shows up there. Your credit score is the grade coaches give after watching that film.

The score is built on a few core factors:

- **Payment history**: Do you pay on time?
- **Credit utilization**: How much of your available credit are you using?
- **Length of credit history**: How long have you been using credit?
- **New credit**: How often do you apply for more?
- **Credit mix**: Do you handle different types of credit responsibly?

In wrestling terms, this is positional trust.

When you stay in good position, defend well, and do not give up easy points, trust builds. When you reach, stall, or give up takedowns, trust disappears quickly.

You cannot talk your way into a better score. You earn it rep by rep.

Credit Is Trust, Not Power

A lot of athletes misunderstand credit because it feels like power.

A higher limit. More access. Bigger numbers.

But credit is not power. It is trust extended conditionally.

The bank is saying, "We believe you can handle this leverage without losing control."

That trust can be removed faster than it is earned.

Late payments, high balances, and careless applications are like giving up back points. One mistake might not end the match, but repeated ones will.

Credit Cards, Loans, and Interest

Credit cards and loans are tools.

They are not inherently good or bad. Like leverage, they depend on how you use them.

Credit cards offer short-term flexibility. They can help smooth cash flow. They can provide protections and rewards. They can also become one of the most expensive habits you ever develop.

Interest is the cost of borrowing. It is your opponent scoring points while you are stuck underneath.

If you carry a balance, interest works against you every single day. The longer you stay there, the harder it becomes to escape. That is why high-interest debt feels suffocating. You are fighting uphill with fatigue setting in.

Loans work the same way, just on a longer timeline. Car loans. Student loans. Personal loans. Mortgages. Each has different rates, terms, and consequences.

Borrowing should always answer one question:

Does this leverage improve my position, or does it expose me?

Good Debt vs Bad Debt

Not all debt is equal.

Good debt helps you build something that creates future options. It has a clear purpose and a long-term payoff.

Examples may include:

- Education that increases earning potential
- A reasonably priced home you can afford comfortably
- A business investment with a clear plan

Bad debt finances consumption. Comfort. Status. Convenience.

Examples include:

- Carrying credit card balances for lifestyle spending
- Financing depreciating items with no plan
- Borrowing because "I can" instead of because it fits

In wrestling terms, good debt is using leverage to advance position. Bad debt is reaching for a move that looks good but leaves you exposed.

The interest rate matters, but it is not the only factor. The real question is whether the debt creates future strength or future pressure.

The Confidence Trap Athletes Fall Into

Athletes are conditioned to believe they can recover.

That confidence wins matches. Financially, it can create blind spots.

Many wrestlers assume future income will fix today's decisions. "I'll pay it off later." "This won't matter long-term." "I can handle it."

Debt does not care how confident you are. It only cares how consistently you pay.

Small balances feel manageable. Minimum payments feel harmless. Over time, momentum shifts. Flexibility disappears. Options shrink.

That is how people get pinned without realizing they were in danger.

Debt Mistakes That Pin You Early

Most debt problems come from the same mistakes.

- **Using credit to fund lifestyle**
- **Ignoring balances because payments feel small**
- **Only looking at monthly payments instead of total cost**
- **Co-signing without understanding the risk**
- **Using debt to avoid discomfort instead of solving problems**

Co-signing deserves special attention.

When you co-sign, you are not helping someone. You are taking full responsibility if they cannot pay. Their mistake becomes your pin.

In wrestling terms, this is putting yourself in danger to save someone else. Noble intentions do not protect you from consequences.

Playing With the Count

Smart wrestlers understand the count.

They know when to attack. They know when to defend. They know when to reset. They do not panic just because the ref starts counting.

Debt requires the same awareness.

Borrowed leverage should be:

- Planned
- Controlled
- Temporary
- Aligned with long-term goals

If debt limits your ability to move, adjust, or breathe financially, you are out of position.

Coach's Perspective

A coach would not sugarcoat this.

Stay in position.

Do not reach.

Do not give up easy points.

Leverage is earned, not abused.

Handle credit with respect or it will handle you.

Match Situations and Decision Points

You can put it on a card. Do you do it because it fits the plan or because it is easy?

You qualify for a loan. Do you ask if you should take it, or just if you can?

Someone asks you to co-sign. Do you understand the worst-case scenario, or are you reacting emotionally?

These are match-deciding moments. Awareness matters more than confidence.

Common Wrestler Mistakes and Financial Parallels

Wrestlers reach under pressure.

Financially, that looks like impulse borrowing.

Wrestlers trust strength over position.

Financially, that looks like overconfidence with debt.

Wrestlers ignore small mistakes.

Financially, that becomes long-term damage.

The patterns are the same. Only the timeline changes.

Winning the Long Match

Borrowed leverage can help you advance or get pinned. The difference is discipline.

You do not need to avoid credit entirely. You need to understand it, respect it, and use it intentionally. Stay in position. Protect flexibility. Do not give up easy points.

That is how you stay on your feet financially.

Athlete Takeaways

- Credit is leverage. Respect it like position.
- Interest is your opponent scoring while you are stuck.
- Borrow to build, not to feel comfortable.
- Small debt mistakes compound into big problems.
- Stay disciplined and do not reach under pressure.

Chapter 5: The Training Room of Money

Banking Basics

Every wrestler knows the importance of the training room.

It is not the spotlight. No crowds. No medals. But if the training room is chaotic, disorganized, or neglected, performance suffers fast. Missed treatment leads to lingering injuries. Poor recovery leads to fatigue. Small issues turn into big problems when you step on the mat.

Your banking system is the training room of your money.

It is where recovery happens. Where preparation lives. Where small issues either get handled early or turn into season-ending problems. Before you worry about investing, growth, or long-term planning, your banking setup has to function cleanly. If the system is sloppy, everything built on top of it becomes unstable.

Checking vs Savings Accounts

Checking accounts are for movement.

Savings accounts are for protection.

That separation matters.

Checking is where money flows in and out. Paychecks hit. Bills get paid. Groceries, gas, and daily spending happen here. It is active. It moves constantly.

Savings is where money sits with purpose. Emergency funds. Short-term goals. Buffers. Protection against the unexpected.

In wrestling terms, checking is live drilling. Savings is recovery and rehab.

If everything is live all the time, you get hurt. If everything is recovery and no drilling, nothing improves. You need both, and you need them clearly separated.

When people blur checking and savings, bad habits form. Spending creeps into money meant for protection. Emergencies turn into credit card problems. Stress increases.

Separation creates clarity. Clarity creates discipline.

Why One Account Is Not Enough

Many athletes keep everything in one account early on. It feels simple.

It is not.

One account makes it hard to tell what money is available to spend and what money is meant to protect you. Every purchase becomes a decision under pressure. Over time, mistakes add up.

A simple structure works better:

- One checking account for income and bills
- One savings account for emergencies
- Optional additional savings for short-term goals

This is not complexity. This is organization.

In wrestling terms, this is knowing your positions. Neutral, top, bottom. When you know where you are, you make better decisions.

Online Banks vs Traditional Banks

Traditional banks offer physical branches, tellers, and face-to-face service. Online banks operate digitally and often provide higher interest rates and lower fees.

There is no universal right answer.

The right bank is the one that fits your system.

Some wrestlers need hands-on coaching. Others thrive with independence and self-management. Banking is the same. What matters is understanding:

- Fees
- Access to cash
- Transfer speed
- Customer support
- Account protections

Online banks often excel at efficiency. Traditional banks often excel at convenience and in-person problem-solving. Many athletes use both.

In wrestling terms, this is choosing the right training environment. The best room is the one that helps you stay consistent and disciplined, not the one with the best reputation.

How Money Moves Electronically

Money does not move instantly just because it is digital.

Direct deposits, transfers, debit transactions, and automatic payments all follow rules and timing windows. Understanding those mechanics keeps you from getting caught off guard.

Paychecks may post early or late. Transfers can take days. Automatic payments may clear before deposits arrive. These timing issues cause overdrafts, fees, and stress when systems are loose.

In wrestling terms, this is mat awareness.

You do not assume you are in bounds. You know where the edge is. Banking requires the same awareness. Knowing when money leaves and when it arrives prevents unnecessary penalties.

Set alerts. Know your balances. Keep buffers. These are defensive habits, not signs of weakness.

Automating Bills and Transfers

Automation is discipline without emotion.

Bills paid automatically prevent missed payments. Automatic transfers build savings without relying on motivation. Systems reduce mistakes because they remove decision-making under fatigue.

In wrestling, conditioning prepares you for late matches. Automation prepares your finances for busy weeks, travel, stress, and distraction.

Automation should include:

- Direct deposit into checking
- Automatic transfer to savings
- Automatic bill payments for fixed expenses

You can still review everything. You just are not relying on memory or willpower.

Protecting Yourself From Fraud

Fraud targets disorganized systems.

Loose accounts. Rarely checked statements. No alerts. No separation.

Protect yourself by:

- Monitoring accounts regularly
- Setting transaction alerts
- Reviewing statements monthly
- Acting immediately on suspicious activity

Fraud is like an illegal move. If you do not call it out, it keeps happening. The faster you respond, the easier it is to fix.

Banks often protect customers who act quickly. Delay creates damage.

Overdrafts and Why They Matter

Overdrafts are not just fees. They are signs of poor positioning.

They happen when timing is off, buffers are too small, or systems are unclear. One overdraft is annoying. Repeated overdrafts damage trust with banks and create unnecessary stress.

Avoid overdrafts by:

- Keeping a buffer in checking
- Separating savings clearly
- Timing bills correctly
- Using alerts

In wrestling terms, this is staying off your back. You might escape once or twice, but living there costs energy and confidence.

The Cost of Ignoring Banking Basics

Most people want to skip banking and jump straight to investing.

That is a mistake.

A weak banking system causes missed opportunities, forced borrowing, and emotional decisions. You end up fixing problems instead of building progress.

Strong banking does not feel exciting because it removes chaos. That is the point.

Coach's Perspective

A coach would be blunt.

Protect the training room.

Details matter.

Handle your business.

Do not create your own problems.

Banking is not optional. It is foundational.

Match Situations and Decision Points

You keep getting hit with fees. Do you fix the system or keep reacting?

You do not know your real balance. Do you check or guess?

You notice a suspicious charge. Do you act immediately or hope it goes away?

Small decisions decide outcomes.

Common Wrestler Mistakes and Financial Parallels

Wrestlers ignore recovery.

Financially, that leads to burnout and mistakes.

Wrestlers trust systems blindly.

Financially, that leads to missed fraud or errors.

Wrestlers avoid boring work.

Financially, that leads to chaos.

The habits transfer.

Winning the Long Season

A clean training room supports everything else. Good banking does not make headlines, but it keeps you organized, protected, and ready to compete.

When your banking system works, money stops feeling overwhelming. You stop reacting and start controlling the match.

That is winning before you step on the mat.

Athlete Takeaways

- Checking is for movement. Savings is for protection.
- Separate systems create discipline and clarity.
- Know how and when your money moves.

- Automation removes mistakes under pressure.
- Protect the system so it protects you.

Part II: Defense, Positioning, and Protection

Position wins matches.

Every wrestler learns this early.

You can be strong. You can be aggressive. You can even score early. But if your positioning is sloppy, none of that matters for long. One bad angle. One careless reach. One moment out of position and you are fighting from underneath, burning energy just to survive.

Defense is not passive.

Defense is control.

In wrestling, good defense keeps you balanced, protects you from bad situations, and puts you in position to score when the opportunity appears. The same is true with money. You cannot build anything lasting if you do not protect what you earn.

Part II of this book is about defense, positioning, and protection. It is about making sure one bad break does not pin you early in the match.

Why Protection Comes Before Growth

Most athletes want to skip defense.

Defense is not flashy. It does not feel like progress. It feels like caution. But every experienced coach knows this truth: offense only works when defense is solid.

Financially, protection does the same job.

Risk awareness, insurance, and conservative assets exist to keep you in the match when life takes an unexpected turn. Medical issues. Accidents. Job loss. Lawsuits. Market downturns. These are not personal failures. They are part of the environment.

Ignoring them does not make you tough. It makes you exposed.

Defense gives you margin. Margin gives you time. Time gives you options.

Positioning Is Everything

In wrestling, position determines leverage.

Being slightly out of position does not always feel dangerous, but it compounds. You give up angles. You lose balance. Suddenly, you are defending instead of attacking.

Money works the same way.

Poor positioning shows up as:

- Too little cash when income changes
- Too much debt when flexibility is needed
- No insurance when risk shows up
- Too much risk for your time horizon

You may feel fine until the moment you are not. Then everything becomes reactive.

Good positioning means your finances are set up so that bad outcomes are survivable, not catastrophic.

Defense Is Not Fear

Many athletes resist financial protection because it feels like playing not to lose.

That is a misunderstanding.

In wrestling, elite defense allows aggressive offense. When you trust your base, your hips, and your positioning, you attack with confidence. When you feel exposed, you hesitate.

Financial defense works the same way.

When you know you have emergency savings, proper insurance, and a realistic understanding of risk, you make better decisions. You are not forcing moves. You are choosing them.

Protection creates freedom.

Controlling the Pace of the Match

Defense controls tempo.

You slow the match when needed. You conserve energy. You prevent desperation situations. You wait for the right opening instead of forcing action.

Money decisions are rarely lost in one dramatic moment. They are lost when people are rushed, stressed, and out of position.

Strong financial defense allows you to:

- Avoid panic selling
- Avoid high-interest debt
- Avoid bad partnerships
- Avoid rushed decisions

You cannot always control what happens. You can control how prepared you are when it does.

What This Section Will Teach You

Part II focuses on four core areas of financial defense:

- **Risk awareness**: understanding when to attack and when to defend
- **Insurance**: protecting against events that can derail progress
- **Income protection**: guarding your earning power
- **Stability assets**: tools that reduce volatility and stress

These chapters are not about maximizing returns. They are about minimizing regret.

Just like wrestling defense, these skills are not exciting to learn, but they are devastatingly effective when needed.

Coach's Perspective

A coach would say it clearly:

Stay in position.

Protect your base.

Do not reach when you do not have to.

Make them earn everything.

Financially, that means respecting risk, protecting income, and refusing to put yourself in unnecessary danger.

The Long View

Championship wrestlers are rarely reckless. They are patient, disciplined, and aware of the match situation at all times.

The same mindset wins financially.

You do not need to dominate every moment. You need to avoid getting pinned by preventable mistakes. Defense keeps you alive long enough to win.

This section is about building a base so strong that when opportunity shows up, you are ready to capitalize instead of scrambling.

Position wins matches.

Protection wins seasons.

Chapter 6: Risk Awareness and Match Strategy

Position wins matches, but strategy decides who controls them.

Opening Story From the Mat

Every wrestler knows this moment.

The match is close. You are tied late in the third period. You feel strong. You feel confident. Your opponent looks tired. The urge hits you hard: attack now. Shoot again. Force something big and finish the match.

But great wrestlers pause.

Not because they are scared.

Because they are aware.

They know the score. The clock. Their gas tank. Their opponent's tendencies. They know whether this is the moment to attack aggressively or stay disciplined, hold position, and wait for a cleaner opening.

Risk in wrestling is never just about the move.

It is about the situation around the move.

Money works the same way.

Most financial mistakes athletes make are not because they are reckless. They happen because risk is misunderstood. People confuse confidence with capacity. Aggression with readiness. Wanting to win with being in position to win.

This chapter is about learning match strategy for money. Knowing when to press and when to protect. When to attack and when to defend.

Emotional Risk vs Financial Risk

In wrestling, emotional confidence matters. You need belief to compete. You need to trust your training and your instincts. But confidence alone does not determine whether a move is smart.

Financially, the same distinction applies.

Emotional risk is how comfortable you feel taking chances.

Financial risk is how much damage you can absorb if things go wrong.

Athletes often have high emotional risk tolerance. You have competed under pressure your entire life. You are used to big moments, close matches, and uncomfortable positions. That builds confidence and toughness.

But financial risk is different.

If one bad outcome would:

- Force you into high-interest debt
- Require selling investments at the wrong time
- Disrupt your career or education
- Create stress that affects performance

Then your financial risk tolerance is lower than your emotional confidence suggests.

In wrestling terms, this is knowing the difference between *wanting the takedown* and *being in position to finish it.* Shooting when your hips are out of position feels aggressive, but it often leads to getting sprawled on and giving up control.

Confidence without awareness leads to bad shots.

The same is true with money.

Time Horizon and Flexibility

Time is one of the most important variables in both wrestling and finance.

In a match, the clock changes everything.

Early in the first period, you can afford to experiment. Late in the third, every move is magnified.

Financially, your **time horizon** matters the same way.

- Money needed soon cannot afford big swings
- Money meant for decades from now can handle volatility
- Short timelines require defense
- Long timelines allow more offense

Flexibility is the hidden factor.

Flexibility means:

- Having savings
- Having stable or predictable income
- Having low fixed obligations
- Having options if something changes

In wrestling, a wrestler with stamina and position can take more chances. A wrestler who is gassed or injured must be more selective.

Money works the same way.

If you have flexibility, you can take calculated risks.

If you do not, you must protect position first.

Ignoring time horizon is like wrestling every match at one speed regardless of score or clock. It looks aggressive, but it loses matches.

How Risk Affects Every Money Decision

Most people think risk only applies to investing.

That is a mistake.

Risk affects **every** financial decision, including:

- How much cash you keep
- How much debt you take on
- What insurance coverage you carry
- How aggressive your lifestyle is
- How concentrated your investments are

Ignoring risk does not make you bold. It makes you vulnerable.

Every financial decision should pass one simple test:

What happens if this does not go my way?

In wrestling terms, that is checking your position before committing to a move. If you cannot defend the counter, you should not attack.

Smart wrestlers think two steps ahead.

Smart financial decisions do the same.

Knowing When to Attack and When to Defend

Great wrestlers understand match flow.

There are moments to attack aggressively:

- When your opponent is off balance
- When you have position and control
- When the risk of giving something up is low

There are also moments to defend:

- When you are ahead
- When you are tired

- When the opponent is baiting you
- When the downside is too large

Money requires the same awareness.

There are times to invest aggressively.

There are times to build cash.

There are times to reduce risk.

There are times to stay patient and do nothing.

The mistake is playing one style all the time.

Always attacking leads to exposure.

Always defending leads to stagnation.

Winning decisions are situational, not emotional.

Coach's Perspective

If a coach were talking about money, the message would sound familiar:

Control what you can control.

Stay in position.

Do not force bad shots.

Make them earn everything.

Win the match one exchange at a time.

Financially, that means:

- Respecting risk
- Matching strategy to your situation
- Avoiding desperation moves
- Staying disciplined under pressure

Risk is part of competition. Poor awareness is optional.

Game Situations and Decision Points

Situation 1:

You hear about a high-risk investment with big upside.

Do you ask if it fits your timeline and flexibility, or just focus on the potential return?

Situation 2:

You want to make a large purchase.

Do you consider how it affects cash flow and flexibility if income changes?

Situation 3:

You feel confident and want to "press."

Do you check downside scenarios, or assume things will work out?

Just like wrestling, the wrong decision at the wrong time changes the match.

Common Athlete Mistakes and Financial Parallels

Athletes trust confidence over position.

Financially, that leads to overexposure.

Athletes attack when tired.

Financially, that leads to stress-driven decisions.

Athletes ignore the clock.

Financially, that leads to poor timing.

The same habits that lose matches lose money.

Winning the Long Game

Risk cannot be eliminated.

Loss can be managed.

The wrestlers who succeed long-term are not reckless. They are disciplined, aware, and patient. They know when to attack hard and when to defend position.

Financial success works the same way.

You do not need to win every exchange. You need to avoid getting pinned by preventable mistakes. Stay in position. Stay flexible. Let opportunity come to you instead of forcing it.

That is not fear.

That is strategy.

Athlete Takeaways

- Position before aggression. Risk only works when you can defend the counter
- Confidence is not the same as capacity. Know the difference
- Time horizon changes the right move
- Flexibility creates options under pressure
- Win money the same way you win matches: awareness, discipline, and patience

Chapter 7: Insurance Fundamentals Every Wrestler Needs

Protection is position. Position keeps you in the match.

Opening Story From the Mat

Every wrestler understands this truth early.

You can do everything right and still get hurt.

You can train year-round, cut weight properly, warm up perfectly, and follow the game plan. One awkward scramble, one slip, one bad landing and the match changes instantly. That reality is why wrestling rooms emphasize prevention, recovery, and preparation. You do not assume injuries will not happen. You assume risk exists and you prepare for it.

Insurance plays that exact role in your financial life.

You do not buy insurance because you expect disaster. You buy it because contact is unavoidable. Life, like wrestling, has pressure, collisions, and unpredictability built into it. Ignoring that does not make you tough. It makes you exposed.

Insurance is not about fear.

It is about staying on the mat.

Why Insurance Is About Staying Available

In wrestling, availability matters more than talent.

It does not matter how good you are if you cannot compete. An injury does not just affect one match. It impacts training, momentum, confidence, and long-term development.

Financially, availability works the same way.

If one unexpected event forces you into debt, wipes out savings, or derails progress, you were not protected. Insurance exists to absorb shocks so you can keep moving forward.

Insurance does not help you score points.

It prevents you from getting pinned by something outside your control.

That is defense.

Health Insurance Basics

Health insurance is non-negotiable.

It covers doctor visits, prescriptions, emergency care, surgeries, and long-term treatment. Without it, one injury or illness can create financial damage that lasts longer than any season.

Wrestlers are used to pain and discomfort. That toughness can become a liability when it leads to avoiding care or skipping coverage. Being tough does not pay medical bills.

In wrestling terms, skipping health insurance is like stepping on the mat without headgear or knee pads. You might be fine for a while. When contact happens, the consequences are real and immediate.

Health insurance is not only about emergencies. It is about access.

Access to preventative care.

Access to early diagnosis.

Access to treatment that prevents small issues from becoming career-ending problems.

Every wrestler should know:

- What plan they have
- What it covers
- What it does not cover
- Their deductible
- Their out-of-pocket maximum

Do not wait until something goes wrong to learn how your coverage works. That is like learning the rules during the match.

Auto and Renters Insurance

Auto and renters insurance are often overlooked, especially by younger athletes.

Auto insurance protects you, your vehicle, and everyone else involved in an accident. It also protects you from lawsuits, medical claims, and long-term financial exposure.

Renters insurance protects your personal property and provides liability coverage if someone is injured in your living space.

In wrestling terms, these policies protect your position off the mat.

You do not need a dramatic event for these to matter. A simple accident, a guest slipping, or damage to property can create legal and financial consequences far beyond the original incident.

Many athletes think, "Nothing bad has happened yet."

That is not a strategy.

Auto and renters insurance are about controlling downside. One mistake should not end the match.

Homeowners Insurance

If you own a home, homeowners insurance is essential.

It protects:

- The structure

- Your belongings
- Liability if someone is injured
- Damage from fire, storms, or accidents

Owning property without insurance is like wrestling without position awareness. Everything feels fine until something breaks loose and you cannot recover.

Homeownership adds responsibility. Insurance is how you manage that responsibility without risking your entire financial future.

This is not optional defense. This is base position.

Deductibles, Premiums, and Coverage Limits

This is where confusion usually starts.

- **Premiums** are what you pay to keep coverage active
- **Deductibles** are what you pay out of pocket before coverage kicks in
- **Coverage limits** are the maximum the policy will pay

Higher deductibles usually mean lower premiums. Lower deductibles usually mean higher premiums. There is no free lunch.

The goal is balance.

You want premiums you can afford consistently.

You want deductibles you can handle without panic.

You want coverage limits that actually protect you when things go wrong.

In wrestling terms, this is conditioning and weight management. Too aggressive in either direction creates risk. Smart preparation keeps you competitive.

Insurance is not about getting every dollar back. It is about preventing financial catastrophe.

Why Being Underinsured Is a Losing Position

Many athletes choose the cheapest policy available without understanding what they are giving up.

That is dangerous.

Saving a small amount on premiums can cost massively when pressure hits. Underinsurance feels smart until it fails under stress.

In wrestling terms, this is cutting too much weight too fast. You might make weight, but you are not strong enough to compete.

Adequate protection beats minimal protection every time.

Coach's Perspective

A wrestling coach would not debate this.

Protect yourself.

Know your position.

Do not leave openings.

Stay available.

Insurance is availability.

If one hit takes you out financially, you were not prepared.

Match Situations and Decision Points

Situation 1:

You are healthy and consider skipping coverage. Do you save money now or protect against inevitable risk?

Situation 2:

You want the cheapest policy possible. Do you understand what happens when something actually goes wrong?

Situation 3:

You assume nothing bad will happen. Are you prepared if it does?

Matches are not lost because of one bad move. They are lost because of repeated exposure.

Common Athlete Mistakes and Financial Parallels

Wrestlers underestimate injury risk.

Financially, that leads to skipping insurance.

Wrestlers focus on toughness instead of protection.

Financially, that leads to underinsuring.

Wrestlers ignore details.

Financially, that leads to surprises at the worst time.

Defense matters even when you feel strong.

Winning the Long Game

Insurance does not win matches.

It keeps you in them.

You cannot control everything that happens. You can control how prepared you are when it does. Strong wrestlers respect defense. Strong financial plans do too.

This is not about playing scared.

It is about staying disciplined.

Athlete Takeaways

- Insurance is position. Protect it
- Health coverage is non-negotiable
- Auto, renters, and homeowners insurance protect your base
- Premiums and deductibles are trade-offs. Know yours
- You cannot win from the sideline. Stay available

Chapter 8: Life, Disability, and Liability Protection

Control the position. Protect the match. Stay in it longer than everyone else.

Every wrestler knows what it feels like when control slips. You are in a good position. You are up on points. Then one small mistake changes everything. A reach instead of solid base. A scramble without awareness. Suddenly you are fighting off your back, burning energy just to survive.

Life works the same way.

Most financial damage does not come from one dramatic event. It comes from exposure. From assuming things will always go according to plan. From believing strength today guarantees safety tomorrow.

Life insurance, disability insurance, and liability coverage exist to protect position when something unexpected happens. They are not exciting. They are not flashy. They do not win matches by themselves.

They prevent you from getting pinned by something outside your control.

Why Protection Beyond Health Insurance Matters

Health insurance covers medical bills.

It does not replace income.

It does not protect your family if you are gone.

It does not shield you from lawsuits or liability claims.

Wrestlers understand layers of defense.

You have stance.

You have hand fighting.

You have hip position.

You have sprawls.

You do not rely on one thing to keep you safe. Financial protection works the same way.

Life, disability, and liability coverage protect different angles of risk. Together, they create control.

Term vs Permanent Life Insurance

Life insurance answers one simple question.

If you were gone tomorrow, who would be financially impacted and for how long?

Life insurance is not about you. It is about everyone who depends on you.

Term Life Insurance

Term life insurance provides coverage for a specific period. Ten years. Twenty years. Thirty years.

If something happens during that term, the policy pays out. If the term ends and nothing happens, coverage ends.

In wrestling terms, term insurance is situational defense. It covers your highest-risk years. When income matters most. When kids are young. When debts exist.

Term insurance is:

- Simple
- Affordable
- Purpose-driven

For most athletes and young families, term insurance is the right starting point.

Permanent Life Insurance

Permanent life insurance lasts for your entire life and includes a savings component.

It is more complex.

It is more expensive.

It is often oversold.

Permanent policies can play a role in advanced planning situations, but they are not automatic upgrades. Buying permanent insurance without understanding it is like trying advanced techniques without mastering fundamentals.

Most wrestlers need position before creativity.

Disability Insurance and Income Protection

If life insurance protects others, disability insurance protects you.

Disability insurance replaces income if you cannot work due to injury or illness.

This matters more than most people realize.

You are far more likely to become disabled during your working years than to die prematurely. One injury, illness, or chronic condition can stop income immediately.

In wrestling terms, this is protecting your ability to compete at all.

You can be mentally sharp.

You can be motivated.

If your body cannot perform, the match stops.

Disability insurance exists to keep cash flow alive when work stops.

Athletes often assume toughness will carry them through. That mindset wins matches. Financially, it creates blind spots.

Key things to understand:

- When benefits start
- How much income is replaced
- How long benefits last
- What qualifies as disability

Disability coverage is one of the most important protections for athletes transitioning into the workforce. Your income is your engine. Protect it.

Umbrella Liability Coverage

Umbrella insurance protects against lawsuits and large liability claims.

If you are sued and damages exceed your auto or homeowners insurance limits, umbrella coverage steps in.

This is protection most people do not think about until it is too late.

In wrestling terms, umbrella coverage is last-resort defense. When everything else is exhausted, it keeps you from getting pinned.

Umbrella coverage matters more as:

- Income increases
- Assets grow
- Public exposure increases
- Family responsibilities expand

It is relatively inexpensive compared to the protection it provides. It is also ignored far too often.

You do not plan to get sued.

You plan for the possibility that someone else might.

Common Insurance Mistakes Athletes Make

Wrestlers make mistakes when they rush positions or ignore fundamentals. Athletes do the same financially.

Mistake 1: Buying Coverage Without Understanding It

If you cannot explain your policy, you do not control it.

Mistake 2: Underinsuring to Save Money

Saving small amounts now can create massive losses later.

Mistake 3: Overbuying Complex Products

Complexity without understanding creates exposure, not protection.

Mistake 4: Ignoring Disability Insurance

Losing income hurts faster than losing assets.

Mistake 5: Assuming "Nothing Will Happen"

That assumption has pinned more athletes financially than any bad investment.

Protection is not pessimism. It is preparation.

Coach's Perspective

A wrestling coach would be blunt.

Protect your base.

Do not reach.

Stay in position.

Win the long match.

Insurance is position control.

You do not win championships by hoping nothing goes wrong. You win by being ready when it does.

Match Situations and Decision Points

Situation 1:

You start earning real income. Do you protect it with disability coverage or assume you will always be able to work?

Situation 2:

You have people depending on you. Do you secure term life insurance or delay because it feels uncomfortable?

Situation 3:

Your assets grow. Do you add umbrella coverage or assume lawsuits only happen to other people?

These decisions do not show up on the scoreboard today. They decide who is still standing later.

Winning the Long Game

Life, disability, and liability insurance do not create wealth.

They protect it.

They keep one event from undoing years of discipline. They allow you to stay composed under pressure. They preserve your ability to keep competing in life after the mat.

Strong wrestlers respect defense.

Strong financial plans do too.

Athlete Takeaways

- Life insurance protects your people, not you
- Disability insurance protects your income engine
- Umbrella coverage protects against worst-case scenarios
- Cheap protection often becomes expensive later
- Control position and you stay in the match

Part III: Controlling the Mat (Investing Fundamentals)

Control beats chaos.

In wrestling, chaos favors the desperate.

Scrambles look exciting. Crowd noise rises. Arms and legs fly. But the wrestler who wins most often is not the one moving the fastest. It is the one who understands position, pressure, and leverage. Control slows the match down. Control forces mistakes. Control lets you dictate where the next exchange happens.

Investing works the same way.

Most people lose money not because markets are rigged or because they lack intelligence, but because they let chaos dictate decisions. Headlines create panic. Friends create FOMO. Short-term moves feel urgent. Without control, money decisions turn into scrambles, and scrambles exhaust you.

This section is about controlling the mat financially.

Not chasing.

Not guessing.

Not reacting.

Control.

Why Investing Feels Chaotic at First

When you first step into live competition, everything feels fast. The mat feels smaller. The pressure feels heavier. The same happens when athletes first encounter investing.

Markets move daily. Numbers change constantly. Opinions are loud and confident. It feels like everyone else knows something you do not.

But just like wrestling, what looks chaotic from the outside is structured underneath.

There are rules.

There are positions.

There are incentives.

The chaos comes from not knowing where you are or why you are there.

Control begins with understanding the environment, not trying to dominate it.

Position Before Power

Good wrestlers do not rely on strength alone. They fight for position first.

Inside control.

Head position.

Hip alignment.

Once position is established, power becomes effective.

Investing follows the same order.

Before chasing returns, you need structure. Before taking risk, you need stability. Before complexity, you need fundamentals.

That means:

- Understanding how markets work
- Knowing the role of stocks, bonds, and cash
- Accepting volatility as part of the match
- Respecting time as your greatest advantage

Trying to overpower the market without position leads to mistakes. Control creates leverage.

Why Fundamentals Matter More Than Big Moves

Every wrestler knows the danger of abandoning basics.

You might hit a big move once. But if your stance is sloppy and your defense is weak, you will get exposed over time.

Investing is no different.

You do not need the perfect stock.

You do not need secret information.

You do not need to predict markets.

You need fundamentals that hold up under pressure.

Diversification.

Discipline.

Patience.

Consistency.

These are not exciting. They are effective.

Championship wrestlers win because they do the boring things better than everyone else. Long-term investors do too.

Control Reduces Emotional Mistakes

Emotion is where most financial damage happens.

Fear makes people sell at the wrong time.

Greed makes people overextend.

Overconfidence makes people ignore risk.

Control does not eliminate emotion. It limits its influence.

When you have a plan, you do not need to react to every move. When you understand your position, you are less likely to panic during scrambles.

In wrestling terms, control keeps you from giving up points during transitions. You may not score immediately, but you do not get scored on either.

That is how matches are won.

Investing Is Not One Match

Wrestlers understand seasons.

You do not win a career in one tournament. You win by staying healthy, improving gradually, and showing up year after year.

Investing works the same way.

One year does not define success.

One bad stretch does not mean failure.

One great run does not mean mastery.

Control means staying in the match long enough for skill and discipline to matter.

This section focuses on:

- Understanding markets instead of fearing them
- Using risk intentionally instead of emotionally
- Letting compounding work instead of forcing outcomes
- Building wealth through position, not power

Coach's Perspective

A wrestling coach would say it plainly:

Stay in position.

Stop scrambling.

Control the mat.

Make them earn everything.

Financially, the advice is the same.

You do not need to dominate the market. You need to stop beating yourself.

Why This Section Matters

Everything that comes later depends on this.

Advanced strategies fail without fundamentals. Complexity backfires without control. Wealth does not grow in chaos.

This part of the book is about slowing the match down, understanding where you are, and taking control of your financial position one exchange at a time.

Control beats chaos.

Every time.

Chapter 9: How Financial Markets Really Work

Every wrestler remembers the first time they faced someone who felt *different*.

Not stronger.

Not faster.

Just calmer.

You shot in hard, and they sprawled without panic. You tried to scramble, and they stayed heavy. You pushed the pace, and somehow they were always one step ahead. The match did not feel chaotic to them. It felt controlled.

That wrestler understood something you did not yet: **the match has a structure**.

Financial markets work the same way.

From the outside, markets look wild. Prices jump. Headlines scream. People argue constantly about what will happen next. To someone without experience, it feels like chaos. But underneath all that noise is a system that rewards patience, ownership, and discipline.

Once you understand the structure, the game slows down.

How Financial Markets Actually Function

At their core, financial markets exist for one simple reason:

To connect people who need capital with people who have capital.

Companies need money to grow. Governments need money to operate.

Investors provide that money in exchange for ownership or interest.

That is it.

Markets are not casinos. They are not prediction machines. They are not designed to make people comfortable. They are systems for allocating capital over time.

In wrestling terms, the market is the mat.

It does not care who you are.

It does not adjust to your emotions.

It rewards those who understand position and control.

Prices move based on expectations about the future, not just what is happening today. Earnings, interest rates, innovation, demographics, and behavior all influence value. That is why markets move before headlines feel "real."

Trying to outguess every move is like trying to predict every grip exchange. You will exhaust yourself and still get caught out of position.

Stocks, Bonds, and Ownership Explained Simply

Stocks: Ownership

When you buy a stock, you are buying **ownership** in a real business.

That company sells products or services. It hires people. It competes. It makes decisions that affect profitability and growth. When the company does well over time, owners benefit. When it struggles, owners feel it.

In wrestling terms, owning stocks is committing to a long season with a team. You do not judge the outcome on one match. You judge it over many competitions.

Stocks carry higher risk because ownership means exposure. But they also carry higher long-term potential because businesses grow.

Bonds: Lending

Bonds are different.

When you buy a bond, you are lending money to a company or government. In return, you receive interest and the promise of getting your principal back.

Less upside.

More predictability.

In wrestling terms, bonds are defensive positioning. You are not trying to score big. You are trying to stay solid, avoid mistakes, and control exposure.

Why Both Matter

You do not win matches with offense alone. You do not win financially with one asset type either.

Stocks provide growth.

Bonds provide stability.

Cash provides flexibility.

Understanding roles is more important than chasing returns.

Market Cycles and Volatility

Markets move in cycles.

Expansion.

Slowdown.

Decline.

Recovery.

Repeat.

This is not a flaw. It is a feature.

Volatility is movement. It is not failure. Prices move because information changes, expectations shift, and emotions fluctuate.

In wrestling terms, volatility is a scramble.

Scrambles feel dangerous, but they are not automatically bad. They only become problems when you panic, overextend, or abandon fundamentals.

Athletes often mistake discomfort for danger. Seeing red numbers feels like losing, even when nothing permanent has happened.

Permanent loss usually comes from:

- Selling in panic
- Overleveraging
- Abandoning long-term plans
- Chasing quick wins

Markets recover over time. Mistakes made under emotional pressure often do not.

Why Long-Term Ownership Wins

Great wrestlers do not judge themselves by one match.

They judge seasons.

They judge development.

They judge consistency.

Financial markets reward the same mindset.

Ownership over time allows:

- Businesses to compound growth
- Dividends to reinvest
- Innovation to play out
- Economic growth to work in your favor

Trying to time every move is like constantly changing your stance mid-match. You lose balance.

Long-term investors accept volatility as part of the process. Short-term traders often confuse activity with progress.

Long-Term Strategy vs Chasing Quick Wins

Quick wins are seductive.

A hot stock.

A new trend.

A friend's big return.

They feel like opportunities. Most of the time, they are distractions.

In wrestling terms, this is chasing big throws without setup. Sometimes it works. Over time, it costs you matches.

Long-term strategy means:

- Defining your role
- Understanding your risk tolerance
- Allocating assets intentionally
- Staying disciplined when others panic

Quick-win chasing creates:

- Overtrading
- Poor timing
- Emotional decisions
- Burnout

The market does not reward excitement. It rewards endurance.

Coach's Perspective

What would a wrestling coach say about markets?

"Stay in position."

"Stop forcing it."

"Control what you can control."

"Next exchange."

"Do not beat yourself."

Financially, that means:

- Do not react to noise
- Do not abandon your plan
- Do not chase what you do not understand
- Stay disciplined

Championship wrestlers win because they do not panic in bad positions. Good investors survive volatility the same way.

Game Situations and Decision Points

Situation 1:

Markets drop sharply. Headlines scream recession. Your account value falls.

Do you:

- Panic and sell?
- Or remember that volatility is normal and stay disciplined?

Situation 2:

A friend brags about a huge return in a short period.

Do you:

- Chase without understanding?
- Or stick to your strategy?

Situation 3:

You feel bored because progress feels slow.

Do you:

- Add unnecessary risk?
- Or trust the process?

Each choice reflects whether you control the mat or let chaos control you.

Common Athlete Mistakes and Financial Parallels

Wrestling Mistake: Panicking in scrambles

Financial Parallel: Panic selling during volatility

Wrestling Mistake: Forcing big moves

Financial Parallel: Chasing hot investments

Wrestling Mistake: Ignoring fundamentals

Financial Parallel: Overcomplicating strategy

The same behaviors that lose matches lose money.

Winning the Long Game

Markets are not opponents to defeat. They are environments to navigate.

You do not need to outsmart everyone.

You do not need perfect timing.

You do not need constant action.

You need discipline, patience, and control.

Just like wrestling, success comes from understanding position, staying composed, and letting time work in your favor.

Athlete Takeaways

- The market is structured, not random. Learn the system before reacting
- Stocks are ownership, bonds are defense. Know their roles
- Volatility is a scramble, not a loss
- Long-term ownership beats chasing quick wins
- Control the mat financially and let others make mistakes

Chapter 10: Risk, Return, and the Power of Compounding

Every wrestler learns this lesson early.

You can shoot aggressively, push the pace, and chase points, but every move comes with exposure. Reach too far on a single leg and you risk getting sprawled on. Go for a big throw without position and you might end up on your back. Wrestling rewards aggression, but only when it is controlled.

The best wrestlers understand **risk management**.

They know when to attack.

They know when to defend.

They know when to stay patient and let the match develop.

Money works the same way.

Risk and return are inseparable. You cannot grow without taking risk, but unmanaged risk ends matches early. Compounding is what turns small, disciplined advantages into long-term dominance, but only if you stay on the mat long enough for it to work.

This chapter is about understanding risk the way elite wrestlers do, not emotionally, not recklessly, but strategically.

Risk and Reward Tradeoffs

There is no reward without risk.

In wrestling, scoring points requires engagement. If you never take a shot, you never score. But if you shoot without setup, without position, you get punished.

Financially, higher potential returns usually require higher risk. Stocks have higher long-term growth potential than bonds, but they fluctuate more. Safer investments feel more stable, but they grow slower.

In wrestling terms:

- High-risk moves are high-reward throws
- Low-risk moves are solid positioning and riding time

Neither is "better" on its own. What matters is **when** and **how** you use them.

Great wrestlers do not wrestle every match the same way. They adjust based on:

- Opponent
- Score
- Period
- Conditioning
- Situation

Smart investors do the same. Risk should match your:

- Time horizon
- Income stability
- Flexibility
- Financial goals

The mistake is treating risk like a personality trait instead of a situational decision.

Emotional Risk vs Financial Risk

This is where athletes often get tripped up.

Emotional risk is how comfortable you *feel* taking chances.

Financial risk is how much damage you can actually absorb.

Wrestlers are conditioned to embrace discomfort. You have pushed through pain, fatigue, and pressure. That builds confidence, which is a strength. But financially, confidence does not replace capacity.

If one bad outcome would:

- Force you into debt
- Require selling investments at the worst time
- Disrupt your life or career

Then your financial risk capacity is lower than your emotional confidence suggests.

In wrestling terms, this is the difference between *wanting* to scramble and being in position to scramble safely.

Elite wrestlers know when their base is strong enough to open up. Financially, that base is savings, stable income, and margin.

Volatility vs Permanent Loss

Volatility scares people because it looks like failure.

Prices go up and down. Accounts fluctuate. Red numbers appear. Emotion kicks in.

But volatility is not the enemy.

Volatility is movement.

Permanent loss is damage.

In wrestling terms:

- Volatility is a scramble
- Permanent loss is getting pinned

Scrambles are uncomfortable. They feel chaotic. But if you stay composed, maintain position, and trust fundamentals, you often come out fine.

Permanent loss usually happens when:

- You panic and abandon position
- You overextend chasing a reversal
- You quit defending

Financially, permanent loss often comes from:

- Panic selling during downturns
- Overleveraging with debt
- Chasing returns without understanding risk

Markets have always recovered over time. Investors who exit emotionally often lock in losses that did not need to exist.

Discomfort is not danger. Losing control is.

Compounding Over Time

Compounding is the most powerful force in finance, and one of the most misunderstood.

Compounding means your gains begin to generate their own gains. Growth builds on growth. Progress accelerates over time, not because you do something different, but because you stay consistent.

Wrestlers understand this instinctively.

Conditioning does not improve from one hard practice. It improves from thousands of reps, meals eaten right, recovery managed well, and showing up day after day.

In wrestling terms, compounding is:

- Mat time
- Strength development
- Technique refinement
- Mental toughness

None of it feels dramatic in the moment. Over years, it separates champions from everyone else.

Financially, compounding rewards:

- Early starts
- Consistency
- Patience
- Staying invested

The longer money stays invested, the more time compounding has to work. That is why time matters more than brilliance.

Why Small Consistent Wins Beat Big Moves

Many athletes believe big outcomes require big moves.

That mindset wins matches sometimes. It loses careers often.

In finance, small consistent actions outperform flashy decisions:

- Regular investing beats trying to time the market
- Staying invested beats jumping in and out
- Simple strategies beat complex ones over time

In wrestling, the best competitors score through:

- Pressure
- Position
- Wear-down
- Discipline

Not constant highlight throws.

Compounding turns discipline into advantage. It does not care about motivation. It rewards repetition.

The Real Cost of Waiting

Waiting feels safe.

"I'll start when I make more."

"I'll invest when things settle down."

"I'll figure it out later."

This is one of the most expensive decisions athletes make.

Time is the one variable you cannot recover.

In wrestling terms, skipping offseason training puts you behind before the season even starts. No amount of effort later fully replaces lost reps.

Financially, every year you wait:

- Reduces compounding
- Increases pressure
- Requires more risk later

Starting small beats starting late.

You do not need perfect conditions. You need consistency.

Coach's Perspective

What would your wrestling coach say about risk and compounding?

"Control what you can control."

"Stay in position."

"Do not force it."

"Next exchange."

"Trust your training."

Financially, that translates to:

- Do not chase what you do not understand
- Accept volatility as part of the match
- Stay disciplined during discomfort
- Let time work

Championship wrestlers trust preparation. Smart investors trust process.

Game Situations and Decision Points

Situation 1:

Markets drop and your account value falls.

Do you:

- Panic and sell to stop the pain?
- Or recognize volatility and stay disciplined?

Situation 2:

You feel behind financially.

Do you:

- Take on extra risk chasing returns?
- Or stay patient and consistent?

Situation 3:

You want to wait until you feel more confident.

Do you:

- Delay and lose time?
- Or start small and build momentum?

Each decision determines whether compounding works for you or against you.

Common Athlete Mistakes and Financial Parallels

Wrestling Mistake: Forcing moves out of position

Financial Parallel: Over-risking without a base

Wrestling Mistake: Panicking in scrambles

Financial Parallel: Selling during volatility

Wrestling Mistake: Skipping fundamentals

Financial Parallel: Ignoring savings and discipline

The habits that lose matches lose money.

Winning the Long Game

Risk is unavoidable. Loss is not.

The athletes who succeed financially understand that:

- Growth requires risk
- Discipline limits damage
- Time magnifies effort

You do not need to win every exchange. You need to stay in the match.

Compounding rewards those who show up, stay patient, and refuse to panic. That is not passive. That is controlled aggression.

Athlete Takeaways

- Risk and reward are always connected. Choose risk intentionally
- Volatility is a scramble, not a pin
- Compounding rewards consistency, not flash
- Waiting costs more than small mistakes
- Stay in position and let time work for you

Chapter 11: Stocks Without the Hype

Every wrestler knows this moment.

You are down late in the match. The crowd is loud. The coach is yelling for action. Your body is tired. You feel pressure to make something happen. That is when inexperienced wrestlers force moves. Big throws. Desperation shots. Anything to change the outcome quickly.

Sometimes it works.

Most of the time, it backfires.

Elite wrestlers understand a hard truth: **forcing highlights loses matches**. Wins come from position, pressure, fundamentals, and patience. You score by staying disciplined long enough for the opening to appear.

Stocks are treated the same wrong way.

People chase headlines. Hot tips. Big stories. "This stock is going to explode." The hype feels urgent, just like a late-match scramble. But investing success does not come from desperation moves. It comes from understanding what you actually own and staying disciplined long enough for it to work.

This chapter strips away the noise and explains stocks the same way wrestling teaches technique. No hype. No shortcuts. Just fundamentals.

What Owning Stock Actually Means

When you buy a stock, you are not buying a lottery ticket.

You are buying **ownership**.

That ownership represents a real business that:

- Sells products or services
- Employs people
- Competes in a market
- Makes decisions that affect profits

Owning stock means you participate in that company's long-term success or failure.

In wrestling terms, owning stock is stepping onto the mat, not cheering from the stands. You are part of the match. Results come from execution over time, not one move.

This is where many investors go wrong. They treat stocks like price movements instead of businesses. They obsess over daily changes instead of long-term fundamentals.

Great wrestlers do not judge performance on one exchange. Great investors do not judge success on one day.

Why Stocks Feel So Emotional

Stocks move. Prices rise and fall constantly. News, opinions, and social media amplify every movement. Emotion creeps in quickly.

But emotions do not change ownership.

If a stock drops in price, you still own the same business. Nothing changes unless the business itself changes. Panic selling is like stepping out of bounds because you felt uncomfortable in a tie-up.

Discomfort is part of the match.

Stocks reward patience because businesses grow over years, not weeks. If you cannot tolerate movement, you should not expect long-term growth.

Growth vs Value Investing

Two common approaches to stock investing are growth and value. They are not opposites. They are styles.

Growth Investing

Growth investing focuses on companies expected to grow faster than average. These companies often:

- Reinvest profits
- Expand aggressively
- Trade at higher prices relative to earnings

Growth stocks attract attention. They move more. They feel exciting.

In wrestling terms, growth investing is attacking aggressively. High pace. High pressure. More upside, but more exposure if fundamentals are weak.

Value Investing

Value investing focuses on companies that appear undervalued relative to fundamentals. These companies often:

- Generate steady cash flow
- Pay dividends
- Move slower

Value stocks feel boring.

In wrestling terms, value investing is strong base, heavy hands, and pressure. Less flash. More control. Harder to knock off balance.

Championship wrestlers use both styles depending on the situation. Investors should too.

The mistake is believing one style always wins. Balance matters.

Dividends and Total Return

Dividends are cash payments some companies make to shareholders. They provide income while you hold the stock.

Many athletes misunderstand dividends. They think dividends are the goal or that dividend stocks are "safer." That is incomplete thinking.

Dividends are only **part** of return.

Total return includes:

- Price appreciation
- Dividends received

Ignoring either one misses the full picture.

In wrestling terms, total return is the final score, not just takedowns. Riding time, escapes, and reversals all matter.

Some great companies pay no dividends because they reinvest everything to grow. Others pay steady dividends because growth is slower. Neither is automatically better.

What matters is how the investment fits your plan.

Why Chasing Hot Stocks Fails

Hot stocks are tempting.

Everyone is talking about them. Prices move fast. Stories sound convincing. Fear of missing out takes over.

This is late-match desperation disguised as opportunity.

Chasing hot stocks often leads to:

- Buying after big gains
- Selling after losses
- Poor timing driven by emotion

In wrestling terms, this is forcing a throw because the crowd wants action.

Coaches hate it because it ignores position.

Stocks punish emotional decision-making the same way wrestling punishes sloppy technique.

Common Investing Myths Athletes Hear

Athletes hear a lot of bad investing advice, often from confident voices with no real track record.

Myth 1: You Have to Trade Constantly to Win

False.

Most successful investors trade very little. Constant trading increases mistakes, taxes, and stress.

In wrestling terms, this is changing strategy every exchange. It creates chaos.

Myth 2: If the Stock Price Drops, You Failed

False.

Price movement does not equal failure. Poor decisions equal failure.

A temporary drop is a scramble. Selling emotionally creates permanent loss.

Myth 3: Stocks Are Just Gambling

False.

Gambling has no ownership, no long-term expectation, and no discipline. Investing is ownership in productive assets over time.

Treating investing like gambling turns it into gambling.

Myth 4: You Need Insider Information

False.

If insider information were required, markets would not work. Discipline and time matter more than secrets.

Why Discipline Beats Excitement

Wrestling teaches patience.

Matches are won by:

- Pressure
- Conditioning
- Position
- Fundamentals

Not by chasing excitement.

Stocks reward the same traits. Excitement leads to overtrading. Overtrading leads to mistakes. Mistakes compound the wrong way.

The best investors often feel bored. That boredom is a sign the system is working.

Coach's Perspective

What would your wrestling coach say about stock investing?

"Stay in position."

"Do not force it."

"Trust your training."

"Control the match."

"Next move."

Translated financially:

- Own businesses you understand

- Ignore the noise
- Stick to the plan
- Avoid emotional reactions

Coaches do not design strategies around hype. Neither should you.

Game Situations and Decision Points

Situation 1:

A stock you own drops 20%.
Do you:

- Panic and sell because it feels bad?
- Or review why you owned it in the first place?

Situation 2:

A friend tells you about a stock that doubled.
Do you:

- Chase it because you feel behind?
- Or stay disciplined and focused on your plan?

Situation 3:

Your portfolio feels boring.
Do you:

- Add risk for excitement?
- Or recognize boredom as stability?

Every decision either strengthens discipline or weakens it.

Common Athlete Mistakes and Financial Parallels

Wrestling Mistake: Forcing big moves

Financial Parallel: Chasing hype

Wrestling Mistake: Losing position under pressure

Financial Parallel: Panic selling

Wrestling Mistake: Ignoring fundamentals

Financial Parallel: Treating stocks like bets

Championship habits translate. Bad habits translate too.

Winning the Long Game

Stocks are not shortcuts.

They are tools for long-term ownership and growth. Used correctly, they compound quietly. Used emotionally, they create stress and regret.

You do not need to predict markets. You need to stay disciplined.

Just like wrestling, the goal is not to win every exchange. The goal is to control the match long enough to win the outcome.

Athlete Takeaways

- Owning stock means owning real businesses, not headlines
- Growth and value both matter depending on position and timing
- Dividends are part of total return, not the whole story
- Hype leads to forced moves and mistakes
- Discipline and position win long matches

Chapter 12: Bonds and Staying in Position

Every wrestler learns this lesson early.

You can be stronger, faster, and more explosive than your opponent, but if you lose position, none of that matters. One bad reach. One step out of stance. One moment of impatience. Suddenly you are on your back, fighting to survive instead of controlling the match.

Elite wrestlers are obsessed with position.

They understand that matches are not won by constant attacks. They are won by **control**. Strong base. Good balance. Smart pressure. Staying in position long enough to let the match come to you.

Bonds play that same role in your financial life.

They are not flashy. They do not make headlines. They rarely produce highlight-reel moments. But they do something far more important. They keep you in position when everything else is moving fast.

Stocks create offense. Bonds create stability. And stability is what allows you to stay disciplined when markets get chaotic.

How Bonds Work

At their core, bonds are simple.

When you buy a bond, you are **lending money**.

You lend money to:

- Governments
- Companies
- Municipalities

In return, you receive:

- Regular interest payments
- The return of your original money at maturity

That is it.

You are not buying ownership like with stocks. You are acting as a lender.

In wrestling terms, bonds are not attacks. They are **base position**. You are not trying to score quickly. You are controlling the mat, conserving energy, and limiting exposure.

This difference matters. Stocks participate in upside and downside. Bonds are designed to provide predictable income and return of principal, assuming the borrower can pay.

Why Bonds Feel Boring (And Why That Is a Good Thing)

Many athletes dismiss bonds because they feel slow.

They do not move like stocks.

They do not excite conversations.

They do not produce bragging rights.

But boredom in finance often equals discipline.

In wrestling, holding center mat is boring to watch. It does not get cheers. But it wins matches. Bonds serve the same function. They stabilize your financial stance so you are not reacting emotionally when markets move.

If everything in your portfolio is aggressive, every downturn feels like a scramble. Bonds reduce that chaos.

Interest Rate Risk Explained Through Wrestling

Interest rate risk is one of the main risks bonds face.

When interest rates rise, existing bonds with lower rates become less attractive, so their prices fall. When rates fall, existing bonds with higher rates become more valuable.

This is not personal. It is mechanical.

In wrestling terms, interest rate risk is **match tempo**. When the pace changes, certain positions become harder to hold. A stance that works at one speed may struggle at another.

Longer-term bonds are more sensitive to interest rate changes. Shorter-term bonds are less sensitive.

The key lesson is awareness, not fear. You do not avoid position because the match might speed up. You adjust your strategy.

Credit Risk and Trust on the Mat

Credit risk is the risk that the borrower cannot repay the bond.

Not all borrowers are equal.

Some are highly reliable, like governments.

Some are solid companies with strong balance sheets.

Others are weaker and must pay higher interest to attract lenders.

Higher interest usually means higher risk.

In wrestling terms, this is trust.

If you wrestle someone disciplined and predictable, you can apply steady pressure. If you wrestle someone reckless, every exchange carries more danger.

Chasing higher bond yields without understanding credit risk is like wrestling someone wild without a plan. You might score, or you might get caught.

When Bonds Make Sense

Bonds are not for everyone at every stage, but they play an important role.

Bonds tend to make sense when:

- You need stability
- You want income
- You are closer to needing the money
- You want to reduce overall portfolio swings

For younger athletes with long time horizons, bonds may play a smaller role. For older athletes or those nearing major financial transitions, bonds become more important.

In wrestling terms, this is adjusting match strategy based on period, score, and conditioning. You do not wrestle the first period the same way you wrestle the third.

Bonds as Emotional Control

One of the most underrated benefits of bonds is emotional.

Bonds reduce volatility in a portfolio. That reduction makes it easier to:

- Stay invested
- Avoid panic selling
- Stick to the plan

This matters more than people realize.

Many investors fail not because of bad investments, but because of bad reactions. Bonds act like a strong base that keeps you grounded when the match gets wild.

You cannot execute if you are constantly off balance.

Bonds in a Diversified Portfolio

Diversification means different assets doing different jobs.

Stocks drive growth.

Bonds provide stability.

Cash provides flexibility.

Bonds are not meant to outperform stocks over long periods. They are meant to **support** them.

In wrestling terms, bonds are the hips and stance that allow your offense to work. Without them, every attack risks putting you out of position.

A diversified portfolio uses bonds to:

- Reduce volatility
- Provide income
- Protect against certain downturns
- Create balance

Balance beats aggression over long careers.

Coach's Perspective

What would your wrestling coach say about bonds?

"Stay in position."

"Don't get reckless."

"Protect your base."

"Control the mat."

"Win the long match."

Translated financially:

- Do not build a portfolio you cannot emotionally handle
- Use bonds to stabilize your approach
- Avoid overexposure
- Respect the role each asset plays

Coaches do not care about flash. They care about results.

Game Situations and Decision Points

Situation 1:

Markets drop sharply and stocks swing wildly.
Do you:

- Panic and abandon your plan?
- Or rely on your stable positions to stay disciplined?

Situation 2:

You approach a major life transition.
Do you:

- Keep everything aggressive?
- Or shift toward more stability?

Situation 3:

Interest rates change.
Do you:

- Overreact?
- Or adjust calmly and stay focused on the long term?

Smart decisions come from awareness, not emotion.

Common Athlete Mistakes and Financial Parallels

Wrestling Mistake: Over-attacking and losing base
Financial Parallel: Overweighting aggressive assets
Wrestling Mistake: Ignoring match situation
Financial Parallel: Ignoring time horizon

Wrestling Mistake: Letting frustration drive decisions
Financial Parallel: Panic selling
Discipline translates. So does impatience.

Winning the Long Game

Bonds will never make you feel like a hero.

They will not give you bragging rights.

They will not dominate conversations.

They will not produce instant wins.

But they do something more important.

They keep you in the match.

Wrestling careers are built on position, discipline, and endurance. Financial lives are no different. Bonds help you stay balanced long enough for your offense to work.

That is how championships are won.

Athlete Takeaways

- Bonds are about control, not excitement
- Interest rate and credit risk matter, but awareness beats fear
- Bonds help you stay disciplined when markets get wild
- Stability supports long-term growth
- Stay in position and let the match come to you

Chapter 13: Funds, ETFs, and Team-Style Investing

Every wrestler remembers the first time they realized they could not win alone.

You might have been talented. You might have had a dangerous move or two. But as the season went on, you learned something deeper. Championships are not won by one position, one move, or one moment. They are won by systems. Training partners who push you. Coaches who see what you miss. A room full of bodies sharpening each other every day.

Wrestling is an individual sport, but no one succeeds without a team.

Investing works the same way.

Many athletes believe success comes from picking the perfect stock, timing the market, or finding the one move no one else sees. That mindset feels familiar. It mirrors chasing a pin instead of controlling the match.

Funds and ETFs represent team-style investing. You are no longer relying on one athlete to carry the load. You are building depth, balance, and resilience into your financial game plan.

What Funds and ETFs Actually Are

At a basic level, mutual funds and ETFs pool money from many investors and use it to buy a collection of investments.

Instead of owning one stock or one bond, you own **a group**.

That group might include:

- Hundreds of companies
- Different industries
- Multiple countries
- Stocks, bonds, or a mix

In wrestling terms, this is a **deep lineup**. You are not counting on one weight class to win the dual. You are building a roster that can absorb losses, adjust matchups, and still compete.

Funds reduce reliance on single outcomes. That is not weakness. That is strategy.

Mutual Funds vs ETFs

Mutual funds and ETFs are similar, but not identical.

Mutual Funds

- Priced once per day after the market closes
- Often purchased directly through an investment company
- Can be actively managed or index-based

ETFs

- Trade throughout the day like a stock
- Typically have lower costs
- Often index-based

In wrestling terms, both are team systems. The difference is **how they operate**, not what they represent.

Mutual funds are more structured and traditional. ETFs are more flexible and efficient. Neither is inherently better. The right choice depends on how you run your system.

Index vs Active Strategies

This is one of the most misunderstood debates in investing.

Active investing means a manager is trying to beat the market by picking winners and avoiding losers.

Index investing means owning the market as it is, accepting average performance with lower cost and lower effort.

Active strategies are like chasing takedowns constantly. When executed perfectly, they can dominate. When mistimed, they leave you exposed.

Index strategies are like positional control. You may not score quickly, but you stay in good position and let consistency win over time.

Most professional athletes underestimate how hard it is to consistently beat strong competition. Markets are filled with professionals, algorithms, and massive resources. Winning does not come from effort alone.

Index investing accepts reality. It says: stay disciplined, control costs, and trust the system.

Why Fees and Expense Ratios Matter

Fees are the quiet opponent most athletes never see coming.

An expense ratio is the annual cost of running a fund. It may look small, but over time it compounds against you.

High fees reduce returns every year.

Low fees keep more money working for you.

In wrestling terms, fees are like bad habits in practice. One sloppy rep does not matter. Thousands of sloppy reps do.

You do not feel fees the day you pay them. You feel them years later when your progress is smaller than it should be.

Winning investors respect margins. They know small leaks sink ships.

Diversification Without Complexity

Many athletes believe diversification requires complexity.

More accounts.

More strategies.

More opinions.

More action.

That is wrong.

Diversification is about **spreading risk**, not increasing difficulty.

Funds and ETFs allow you to diversify:

- Across companies
- Across industries
- Across countries
- Across asset types

All without managing dozens of individual positions.

In wrestling terms, this is drilling fundamentals instead of inventing new moves. You are not trying to be flashy. You are trying to be effective.

Complexity often creates confusion. Confusion leads to mistakes. Simple systems are easier to execute under pressure.

Why Team-Style Investing Fits Athletes

Athletes thrive in systems.

You understand roles.

You respect structure.

You know repetition matters.

You know results come from consistency, not chaos.

Funds and ETFs reward those exact traits.

You are not guessing.

You are not reacting daily.

You are not chasing rumors.

You are executing a plan.

That discipline is familiar. It is what made you successful on the mat.

The Emotional Advantage of Funds

One of the biggest benefits of funds and ETFs is emotional protection.

When you own one stock, every headline feels personal.

When you own hundreds, noise matters less.

Losses in one area are balanced by strength in another.

In wrestling terms, this is confidence in your conditioning. You do not panic after one scramble because you trust your base.

Funds create emotional distance between you and daily market drama. That distance protects discipline.

Coach's Perspective

What would your coach say?

"Trust the system."

"Do not try to win every exchange."

"Stay patient."

"Control what you can control."

"Reps matter."

Translated financially:

- Pick a solid structure
- Keep costs low
- Stay diversified
- Execute consistently

Coaches hate freelancing. Markets punish it too.

Game Situations and Decision Points

Situation 1:

You hear about a stock everyone is talking about.
Do you:

- Chase it out of fear of missing out?
- Or stay with your diversified plan?

Situation 2:

Your portfolio has a rough month.
Do you:

- Tinker and over-adjust?
- Or trust the long-term system?

Situation 3:

You are tempted by complexity.
Do you:

- Add layers you cannot manage?
- Or keep the plan executable?

Smart wrestlers win by position. Smart investors win by structure.

Common Athlete Mistakes and Financial Parallels

Wrestling Mistake: Relying on one move
Financial Parallel: Concentrated investing
Wrestling Mistake: Ignoring conditioning
Financial Parallel: Ignoring fees
Wrestling Mistake: Overthinking mid-match
Financial Parallel: Over-managing portfolios

Fundamentals travel across domains.

Winning the Long Game

Very few wrestlers dominate every match with highlights.

Most champions win through:

- Consistency
- Preparation
- Discipline
- Trust in their system

Funds and ETFs embody that approach.

You are not trying to outsmart everyone. You are trying to stay in the match long enough for discipline to compound.

That is how careers are built.

That is how wealth is built.

Athlete Takeaways

- Team-style investing beats solo heroics
- Index strategies reward discipline and patience
- Fees matter more than most people realize
- Diversification protects you from single mistakes
- Trust the system and execute every day

Chapter 14: Real Estate and Alternative Tactics

Every wrestler has a moment when they want to get creative.

Maybe you are tired of grinding through ties. Maybe the match feels slow. Maybe you want to end it early. You start looking for big throws, risky rolls, or moves you have not fully mastered yet. Sometimes it works. When it does, it feels incredible. When it fails, you give up position and spend the rest of the match fighting uphill.

Experienced wrestlers learn a hard truth.

Flashy tactics are tools, not foundations.

Real estate and alternative investments work the same way. They can be powerful. They can change outcomes. But when they are used too early or without understanding, they cost position, flexibility, and control.

These are not your stance and motion. These are situational tactics.

Renting vs Owning

One of the biggest financial decisions athletes face is housing.

Renting provides flexibility.

Owning provides long-term potential.

Neither choice makes you disciplined or irresponsible. Context matters.

Renting is like staying mobile on the mat. You can adjust quickly. You are not locked into one position. You do not carry responsibility for maintenance or unexpected issues. If your income changes, your location changes, or your career moves, renting allows you to adapt without penalty.

Owning is like committing to top position. You gain control. You build equity. But you also accept responsibility. Repairs, taxes, insurance, and time all come with the position.

The mistake athletes make is believing ownership is always a win.

Buying before you are ready is like forcing a pin without control. It looks aggressive, but it often backfires.

Good housing decisions depend on:

- Income stability
- Time horizon
- Location certainty
- Willingness to manage responsibility

There is no trophy for owning early. There is only sustainability.

The Hidden Costs of Ownership

Most people focus on the upside of owning and underestimate the grind.

Ownership includes:

- Maintenance and repairs
- Property taxes
- Insurance
- Unexpected expenses
- Reduced flexibility

In wrestling terms, this is carrying extra weight into a match without preparation. You can survive for a while, but fatigue shows up at the worst time.

Ownership can be a strong long-term move when it fits your life. When it does not, it becomes a distraction that drains energy and resources.

Position only matters if you can hold it.

REITs and Indirect Ownership

Real Estate Investment Trusts, or REITs, offer a different way to access real estate.

Instead of owning property directly, you own shares in companies that own and operate real estate. You get exposure to income and potential growth without dealing with tenants, repairs, or leverage.

In wrestling terms, this is controlling the center of the mat without overcommitting. You stay involved without taking unnecessary risk.

REITs can:

- Provide income
- Add diversification
- Preserve liquidity

They also come with market risk. Prices fluctuate. Income can change. They are not guaranteed.

For many athletes, REITs make more sense early than direct ownership because they keep systems simple and flexible.

You stay in position without getting pinned by responsibility.

Alternatives Like Commodities and Private Investments

Alternative investments include:

- Commodities
- Private equity
- Private credit
- Hedge strategies
- Other non-traditional assets

They sound sophisticated. They often feel exclusive. That is part of the appeal.

In wrestling terms, these are advanced tactics. They can be effective, but only when fundamentals are locked in.

Alternatives are often:

- Illiquid
- Hard to value
- Expensive
- Complex
- Difficult to exit

Athletes are drawn to alternatives because they feel like an edge. That mindset is familiar. You have spent your life chasing advantages. Financially, that instinct needs discipline.

Using alternatives before you understand them is like attempting a high-risk throw without drilling it. The margin for error is small, and the consequences are large.

Liquidity and Risk Considerations

Liquidity is how quickly you can access your money.

Cash is liquid.

Public stocks and bonds are generally liquid.

Real estate and private investments often are not.

Illiquidity is not inherently bad. It just needs to be respected.

In wrestling terms, liquidity is your ability to reset position. If you are locked into a bad spot, options disappear.

Before committing to illiquid investments, ask:

- When might I need this money?
- What happens if income changes?
- What if life forces an adjustment?

Ignoring liquidity is one of the fastest ways athletes lose control of their finances.

Why Alternatives Are Often Used Too Early

Alternatives appeal to ego.

They sound advanced.

They sound wealthy.

They sound like what successful people do.

That attraction leads athletes to skip steps.

In wrestling, you do not learn advanced tactics before mastering stance, balance, and defense. Financially, the same rule applies.

Alternatives should complement a strong foundation, not replace it.

If your budget is unstable, savings are thin, and investing basics are not established, alternatives add risk, not opportunity.

Control beats chaos.

The Difference Between Strategy and Distraction

There is nothing wrong with real estate.

There is nothing wrong with alternatives.

The issue is timing and intention.

Strategy fits into a plan.

Distraction pulls you away from it.

Ask yourself:

- Does this strengthen my position?
- Or does it complicate my system?

Champions know when to attack and when to stay disciplined.

Coach's Perspective

What would your coach say?

"Position before submission."

"Do not force it."

"Stay patient."

"Win the hand fight."

"Control the match."

Translated financially:

- Master fundamentals first
- Respect risk and liquidity
- Do not chase excitement
- Build from strength

No coach installs advanced tactics before basics are automatic.

Game Situations and Decision Points

Situation 1:

You want to buy property because it feels like the next step.

Do you:

- Evaluate income stability and flexibility?
- Or buy because it sounds responsible?

Situation 2:

You hear about a private deal with high returns.

Do you:

- Ask about liquidity, risk, and structure?
- Or trust the hype?

Situation 3:

You feel bored with steady progress.

Do you:

- Add complexity?
- Or stay disciplined?

Matches are won through awareness, not impulse.

Common Athlete Mistakes and Financial Parallels

Wrestling Mistake: Forcing big moves

Financial Parallel: Premature alternatives

Wrestling Mistake: Ignoring position

Financial Parallel: Ignoring liquidity

Wrestling Mistake: Chasing highlights

Financial Parallel: Chasing complexity

Fundamentals win when pressure rises.

Winning the Long Game

Real estate and alternatives can play a role in a strong financial plan. They are not shortcuts.

They require patience.

They require understanding.

They require discipline.

Just like wrestling, the goal is not to win one scramble. It is to control the match from start to finish.

Stay in position.

Protect flexibility.

Layer tactics only when the foundation is secure.

That is how long seasons are won.

Athlete Takeaways

- Renting and owning are tools, not trophies
- REITs offer exposure without operational stress
- Alternatives add complexity and risk
- Liquidity protects flexibility under pressure
- Master fundamentals before advanced tactics

Part IV: Match Management and Adjustments

Championships are won through preparation and adjustments.

No wrestling match goes exactly as planned.

You study film. You drill positions. You know your opponent's tendencies. Then the whistle blows, and reality shows up. The pace is different. The strength feels heavier. The timing is off. What wins matches is not the original plan alone, but your ability to adjust without panic.

Money works the same way.

You can build a solid financial foundation and still run into unexpected situations. Markets move. Jobs change. Income fluctuates. Life hits you with injuries, opportunities, and curveballs you did not see coming. Winning financially is not about predicting everything perfectly. It is about managing the match as it unfolds.

This part of the book is about staying composed, making smart adjustments, and protecting position over the long season.

Preparation Creates Options

In wrestling, preparation does not guarantee victory, but it gives you options.

When you are in shape, you can push the pace or slow it down. When your defense is solid, you can take calculated risks. When your fundamentals are sharp, mistakes do not spiral into losses.

Financial preparation works the same way.

Savings give you breathing room.

Diversification gives you flexibility.

Clear systems give you confidence.

Without preparation, every challenge feels urgent. With preparation, challenges become manageable.

Most financial mistakes are not caused by bad intentions. They are caused by being unprepared and reacting emotionally.

Adjustments Without Overreaction

One of the hardest lessons for wrestlers is learning not to overreact.

You give up a takedown. The match is not over.

You get warned for stalling. You adjust your pace.

You lose the first period. You stay composed.

The same discipline is required with money.

Markets drop. That does not mean your plan failed.

Expenses increase. That does not mean you abandon savings.

Life changes. That does not mean you blow up your system.

Smart adjustments are measured, not emotional. They are based on facts, not fear.

Champions adjust between periods. They do not reinvent themselves mid-match.

Managing the Clock and the Score

Every match has a clock and a score. Good wrestlers always know both.

If you are ahead, you protect position.

If you are behind, you press intelligently.

If time is short, decisions matter more.

Financially, time and score matter too.

Your time horizon determines how much risk you can take.

Your current position determines how aggressive or defensive you should be.

Someone early in their career with flexibility can afford different risks than someone close to a major financial goal. Ignoring the clock leads to forced decisions. Ignoring the score leads to unnecessary exposure.

Awareness wins matches.

Avoiding Ego-Driven Decisions

Ego costs wrestlers matches.

Trying to prove toughness instead of scoring.

Forcing a move because the crowd is watching.

Refusing to adjust because "this always works."

Money punishes ego the same way.

Chasing returns to look smart.

Holding losing positions to avoid admitting mistakes.

Taking risks that do not fit your situation.

Winning financially requires humility. The willingness to make boring adjustments. The discipline to stick with what works, even when it is not exciting.

Preparation plus humility beats raw confidence every time.

Staying Disciplined During Long Seasons

Wrestling seasons are long. Financial seasons are longer.

There will be stretches where progress feels slow. Times when effort does not show immediate results. Moments when comparison creeps in and patience fades.

This is where systems matter.

Rebalancing instead of guessing.

Reviewing instead of reacting.

Adjusting intentionally instead of emotionally.

Discipline keeps you in position when others burn out.

Coach's Perspective

What would your coach say?

"Stay in position."

"Trust your training."

"Make the adjustment."

"Do not beat yourself."

"One match at a time."

Financially, that means:

- Prepare before pressure hits
- Adjust without panic
- Respect the clock
- Protect your base

Championships are not won with one big move. They are won through steady control.

Winning the Long Season

This part of the playbook is about maturity.

Understanding that no plan stays perfect.

Accepting that adjustments are part of the process.

Staying disciplined when emotions rise.

In wrestling and in money, the athletes who win are not the ones who never get out of position. They are the ones who know how to get back without giving up the match.

Preparation gives you confidence.

Adjustments keep you competitive.

Discipline finishes the job.

That is match management.

Chapter 15: Asset Allocation and Match Control

Every experienced wrestler knows this truth.

You do not win matches by attacking nonstop. You win by controlling position.

You manage distance. You know when to pressure forward and when to settle your base. You understand when to shoot, when to sprawl, and when to stay patient in the center of the mat. Wrestlers who chase points recklessly get countered. Wrestlers who control position dictate the match.

Asset allocation is match control for your money.

It determines how aggressive or defensive you are, how much risk you can absorb, and how well you stay composed when conditions change. Most financial mistakes happen not because someone chose bad investments, but because their overall positioning was wrong for their situation.

What Asset Allocation Really Means

Asset allocation is how you divide your money among different types of investments.

Primarily:

- Stocks for growth
- Bonds for stability
- Cash for flexibility

In wrestling terms, asset allocation is how you balance offense, defense, and position awareness.

Too much offense with no defense leaves you exposed.

Too much defense with no offense leaves you stuck.

No awareness of position leads to mistakes under pressure.

Your allocation is not about predicting outcomes. It is about controlling risk so you can stay in the match regardless of what happens next.

Stocks, Bonds, and Cash: Controlling the Mat

Stocks are your offense.

They drive growth. They push the pace. They create scoring opportunities over time. Stocks are volatile, just like aggressive attacks. They create movement, but they also create exposure if you are out of position.

Bonds are your defense.

They slow the match down. They absorb impact. They provide structure when things get chaotic. Bonds do not win matches by themselves, but they keep you from getting pinned when momentum swings.

Cash is your balance and flexibility.

Cash lets you reset. It gives you options. It allows you to react without panic. In wrestling terms, cash is knowing you can disengage, reset your stance, and re-enter under control.

Match control comes from blending all three.

Domestic vs International Exposure: Knowing the Mat You're On

Not every match is the same.

Different refs.

Different styles.

Different environments.

Financial markets work the same way.

Domestic investments focus on companies and economies you are familiar with. International investments expose you to different regions, growth patterns, and risks.

In wrestling terms, this is competing against different styles.

Some opponents rely on strength.

Some rely on speed.

Some rely on technique.

Diversifying across domestic and international markets reduces reliance on one environment. You are not betting your season on one mat, one ref, or one style.

You do not need everything everywhere. You need exposure that supports balance.

Diversification Principles: Position Over Prediction

Wrestlers do not win by predicting every move.

They win by staying in good position so no move beats them clean.

Diversification works the same way.

It spreads risk across:

- Asset types
- Industries
- Regions
- Time

Diversification does not eliminate losses. It prevents one mistake from ending the match.

The goal is not maximum upside. The goal is survival plus progress.

Financially, diversification is refusing to rely on one hold, one setup, or one opponent mistake. It is trusting your system to work across conditions.

Career-Stage Allocation: Wrestling Changes Over Time

No wrestler approaches every season the same way.

A younger wrestler with years ahead can afford to take more risks, experiment with offense, and push the pace. A veteran wrestler understands preservation, positioning, and efficiency.

Your financial career works the same way.

Early career

- Longer time horizon
- Higher ability to recover
- More tolerance for volatility

This allows for heavier stock exposure and growth-focused positioning.

Mid-career

- Competing priorities
- Family, career, major goals
- Less tolerance for big swings

Balance becomes critical. Defense matters more.

Later career

- Capital preservation
- Income needs
- Lower tolerance for mistakes

Position control becomes the priority. Avoiding major losses matters more than chasing points.

Ignoring career stage is like wrestling the same way at 35 as you did at 18. Experience should change strategy.

Why Poor Allocation Breaks Discipline

Most investors fail not because they lack knowledge, but because their allocation does not match their reality.

Too aggressive and fear takes over during downturns.

Too conservative and impatience leads to risky behavior.

When allocation fits your situation, discipline becomes easier. You are not fighting your own emotions every time the match shifts.

Good allocation supports behavior. Bad allocation exposes weakness.

Coach's Perspective

What would your coach say?

"Stay in position."

"Don't chase."

"Control the mat."

"Know the situation."

"Win the match you're in."

Financially, that means:

- Match risk to your reality
- Balance offense and defense
- Respect where you are in your career
- Protect your base before attacking

Championship wrestlers win because they understand positioning, not because they force action.

Game Situations and Decision Points

- Markets drop suddenly. Do you panic, or does your allocation give you confidence to stay composed?
- You hear about a hot investment. Do you chase it, or ask whether it fits

your position?

- Life changes your priorities. Do you adjust your allocation, or ignore the new reality?

These are match decisions. Control matters.

Common Wrestler Mistakes and Financial Parallels

Wrestlers chase points.

Financially, that means chasing returns.

Wrestlers ignore position.

Financially, that means ignoring allocation.

Wrestlers rely on strength alone.

Financially, that means ignoring diversification.

The same mistakes lose matches and money.

Winning the Long Match

Asset allocation is not about brilliance.

It is about control.

It keeps you competitive when conditions change. It allows you to stay disciplined when emotions rise. It helps you win matches you do not dominate.

In wrestling and in money, the athlete who controls position controls the outcome.

Athlete Takeaways

- Control the mat before you chase points
- Balance offense, defense, and flexibility
- Allocate based on your career stage, not your ego
- Diversification protects you when things get chaotic
- Match control wins long seasons

Chapter 16: Buying, Holding, and Staying Disciplined

Every wrestler remembers their first big tournament.

The bracket comes out. You see names. Some you recognize. Some you do not. The temptation is to think ahead, to worry about who you might face later, or to panic about a tough draw. The disciplined wrestler does something different. They focus on the first match. They trust their training. They wrestle their style.

Investing works the same way.

Most people do not lose money because they choose the wrong investment. They lose money because they abandon discipline. They overthink. They react to noise. They try to outsmart the moment instead of trusting the process.

Buying, holding, and staying disciplined is the wrestling equivalent of controlling your match from start to finish.

Opening and Funding Accounts: Getting on the Mat

You cannot win a match you never step into.

Opening an investment account is simply stepping on the mat. It is not glamorous. It does not require perfect timing. It just requires action.

Common accounts include:

- Employer retirement plans

- Individual retirement accounts
- Brokerage accounts

The biggest mistake athletes make is waiting for the "right time" to start. There is no perfect whistle. There is only the moment you begin.

Funding the account is like showing up to practice consistently. One workout does not matter. Regular reps do.

Small, consistent contributions beat large, emotional decisions. Wrestling teaches you that progress comes from showing up day after day, not from one heroic session.

Market Orders vs Limit Orders: Choosing the Right Setup

In wrestling, you do not shoot blindly.

You set things up. You understand position. You know whether you are attacking in motion or from control.

Market orders and limit orders work the same way.

A market order executes immediately at the current price. It prioritizes speed and simplicity.

A limit order sets a specific price and waits until the market reaches it. It prioritizes precision and patience.

Neither is "better" in all situations.

Market orders are like straightforward shots. Simple. Efficient. Executed without hesitation.

Limit orders are like timing a reattack. You wait for the right moment. You accept that it may not happen.

The mistake is not understanding which one you are using and why. Discipline means choosing deliberately, not reacting emotionally.

Buy-and-Hold Discipline: Winning in Overtime

Wrestling matches are rarely decided in the first scramble.

They are decided by conditioning, composure, and the ability to stay disciplined when fatigue sets in. The wrestler who panics late gives up position. The wrestler who stays patient finds openings.

Buy-and-hold investing is the same.

You buy quality investments and hold them through ups and downs. You accept volatility as part of the match. You trust that time favors discipline.

Chasing constant changes is like switching game plans every period. It creates confusion and mistakes.

Markets move.

News changes.

Crowd noise increases.

Holding is not laziness. It is discipline.

It means you believe in your preparation enough to stay the course when discomfort shows up.

Avoiding Emotional Decisions: Staying Composed Under Pressure

Every wrestler faces moments where emotion threatens control.

A bad call.

A missed takedown.

A close score late in the match.

The wrestler who reacts emotionally gives openings. The wrestler who stays composed stays in position.

Money decisions are emotional because money represents security, identity, and future freedom.

Fear shows up during market drops.

Greed shows up during market highs.

Overconfidence shows up after short-term wins.

Emotional investing is like wrestling angry or scared. You stop thinking clearly. You abandon fundamentals.

Discipline is not about ignoring emotion. It is about not letting emotion drive decisions.

Why Discipline Beats Timing

Many athletes believe they can time markets the same way they time a shot.

That belief is dangerous.

Even elite investors struggle to consistently time entry and exit points. Markets are complex. Outcomes are uncertain.

Wrestling teaches a different lesson.

You do not need perfect timing. You need good position.

Consistent investing over time beats trying to jump in and out. Staying invested matters more than guessing right.

Discipline removes the pressure to be perfect.

Coach's Perspective

What would your coach say?

"Trust your training."

"Stay in position."

"Don't flinch."

"One move at a time."

"Finish the match."

Financially, that means:

- Start investing instead of waiting
- Choose simple, repeatable actions
- Hold through discomfort
- Avoid reacting to noise

Coaches do not reward panic. They reward discipline.

Game Situations and Decision Points

- The market drops sharply. Do you sell out of fear or stay in position?
- A hot investment dominates headlines. Do you chase it or stick to your plan?
- You feel bored with steady progress. Do you force action or trust the process?

These moments define outcomes.

Common Wrestler Mistakes and Financial Parallels

Wrestlers rush shots.

Financially, that means impulsive trades.

Wrestlers abandon fundamentals.

Financially, that means selling at the wrong time.

Wrestlers let emotion control effort.

Financially, that means fear and greed driving decisions.

The same lack of discipline costs matches and money.

Winning the Long Match

Investing is not a single bout. It is a season, then a career.

The winners are not the ones who make the flashiest moves. They are the ones who stay disciplined across years of uncertainty.

Buying gets you in the match.

Holding keeps you competitive.

Discipline wins over time.

Just like wrestling.

Athlete Takeaways

- Step on the mat. Waiting doesn't win matches
- Simple setups beat flashy moves
- Hold position when the match gets uncomfortable
- Emotion loses matches. Discipline wins them
- Trust the process and finish strong

Chapter 17: Rebalancing and Between-Period Adjustments

Every wrestler knows the feeling between periods.

You head to the corner. Your lungs are burning. Sweat is dripping. The score is close. Your coach is not reteaching wrestling from scratch. They are making adjustments. Small ones. Grip here. Angle there. Pace needs to change. Protect the lead or open up the attack.

Championships are not won by reinventing yourself every period. They are won by making smart adjustments while staying true to your base.

Rebalancing your investments works the same way.

It is not about chasing what is hot. It is not about panic. It is about restoring position, managing risk, and keeping control as conditions change.

How Often to Review Investments: Checking the Scoreboard

You do not stare at the scoreboard every second of a match.

But you always know the score.

Financially, reviewing investments works the same way. You need awareness, not obsession.

Most athletes either:

- Never look at their portfolio
- Or look constantly and react emotionally

Neither works.

A reasonable review schedule might be:

- Once or twice per year for long-term accounts
- During major life changes
- When goals or timelines shift

In wrestling terms, this is knowing the score at the end of each period, not after every scramble.

Too little awareness leads to drifting out of position. Too much attention leads to overreaction.

What Rebalancing Actually Means

Rebalancing is the act of bringing your portfolio back to its intended position.

Over time, some investments grow faster than others. That growth can quietly change your risk level.

For example:

- Stocks perform well and become a larger portion of your portfolio
- Bonds lag and shrink as a percentage
- Your risk increases without you choosing it

Rebalancing is not about predicting the market. It is about restoring balance.

In wrestling terms, it is regaining center position. You are not chasing points. You are reestablishing control.

Rebalancing Strategies: Small Moves, Big Impact

There are a few common ways to rebalance.

Time-based rebalancing

You adjust on a schedule, such as once per year.

This is like routine between-period coaching. Predictable. Calm. Structured.

Threshold-based rebalancing

You adjust when allocations drift beyond a set range.

This is like reacting when position is clearly compromised. You do not panic, but you act.

Cash-flow rebalancing

You use new contributions to restore balance instead of selling.

This is efficient and disciplined. Like scoring without exposing yourself.

The goal is not perfection. The goal is control.

Life Changes and Portfolio Updates: New Match Conditions

Wrestling changes as the match progresses.

Fatigue sets in.

The opponent adjusts.

The score shifts.

Life does the same thing.

Major life events should trigger a portfolio review:

- Career changes
- Income increases or decreases
- Marriage or divorce
- Children
- Health issues
- Approaching major financial goals

Ignoring these changes is like wrestling the third period the same way you wrestled the first, even though your body and the score are different.

Adjustments are not weakness. They are awareness.

Risk Changes Even When Markets Do Not

One of the biggest mistakes athletes make is assuming risk only changes when markets move.

In reality, risk changes when you change.

A portfolio that made sense at 25 may be dangerous at 45.

A portfolio built for growth may be inappropriate when money will be needed soon.

Rebalancing is how you acknowledge reality without emotion.

In wrestling terms, this is knowing when to protect a lead instead of forcing points.

Avoiding Over-Coaching: When Too Much Adjustment Hurts

Every wrestler has experienced bad coaching.

Too many instructions.

Contradictory advice.

Constant yelling to change strategy mid-move.

It creates hesitation.

Financially, over-coaching shows up as:

- Constant tinkering
- Reacting to headlines
- Switching strategies frequently
- Chasing short-term performance

Over-management feels productive. It is usually destructive.

Rebalancing is intentional. Over-trading is emotional.

The best adjustments are simple and decisive, not constant.

Discipline Over Drama

Rebalancing often requires doing something uncomfortable.

Selling what has done well.

Buying what feels boring.

Ignoring noise.

That discomfort is the price of discipline.

In wrestling, the disciplined athlete stays in position even when the crowd wants action. Financially, discipline means sticking to a plan when excitement tempts you to abandon it.

Coach's Perspective

What would your coach say in the corner?

"Know the score."

"Stay in position."

"Small adjustments."

"Don't get greedy."

"Finish strong."

Translated to money:

- Review, do not obsess
- Rebalance to control risk
- Adjust when life changes
- Avoid unnecessary moves

Great coaches do not panic. Neither should you.

Game Situations and Decision Points

- Your portfolio drifts heavily toward stocks after a strong market. Do you rebalance or let risk creep?
- You change jobs and income jumps. Do you update your strategy or

keep everything the same?
- Markets get volatile. Do you overhaul the plan or make measured adjustments?

These moments define long-term outcomes.

Common Wrestler Mistakes and Financial Parallels

Wrestlers chase points late.

Financially, that means chasing returns.

Wrestlers abandon position under pressure.

Financially, that means abandoning strategy.

Wrestlers listen to too many voices.

Financially, that means reacting to noise.

Control wins matches. Discipline wins financially.

Winning the Long Season

A wrestling season is not won in one match.

It is won through consistency, recovery, and smart adjustments along the way.

Rebalancing keeps you aligned with your goals as conditions change. It protects you from drifting into unnecessary risk. It allows you to stay composed across years, not just moments.

That is how you stay competitive long after others burn out.

Athlete Takeaways

- Check the score, don't stare at it
- Rebalance to regain position, not to chase points
- Adjust when life changes, not just when markets move
- Avoid over-coaching and emotional tinkering
- Discipline between periods wins the match

Chapter 18: The Mental Side of Money

Every wrestler knows this truth.

Matches are often decided before the first takedown.

Not because of strength.

Not because of technique.

But because of mindset.

You can be in incredible shape, drill relentlessly, and know every counter in the book, but if your head is not right, none of it shows up when the whistle blows. Wrestling exposes mental weakness fast. One moment of hesitation. One emotional reaction. One lapse in composure. And suddenly you are fighting uphill.

Money works the same way.

Most financial mistakes are not caused by lack of intelligence. They are caused by fear, greed, overconfidence, and pressure. The mental side of money determines whether good plans are executed or abandoned when it matters most.

Fear, Greed, and Overconfidence: The Big Three

These three emotions show up constantly in wrestling rooms.

Fear shows up when an opponent feels stronger or faster.

Greed shows up when you force a move instead of waiting for position.

Overconfidence shows up when you stop respecting fundamentals.

Financially, these same emotions destroy discipline.

Fear causes panic.

Greed causes chasing.

Overconfidence causes recklessness.

Fear shows up when markets drop. Account balances fall. Headlines scream crisis. People sell at the worst possible moment because discomfort feels like danger.

Greed shows up when things are going well. Hot investments. Big wins. "Everyone is making money." People abandon plans and take on more risk than they can handle.

Overconfidence shows up when past success convinces someone they are immune to mistakes. They stop planning. Stop checking risk. Stop respecting downside.

In wrestling terms, this is wrestling the opponent instead of the match.

Crowd Noise and Pressure

Wrestling teaches you to compete in uncomfortable environments.

Gyms are loud.

Crowds are close.

Opponents talk.

Parents yell.

Coaches shout instructions.

The athlete who wins is the one who can block it out and execute.

Money comes with its own crowd noise.

News cycles.

Social media.

Friends bragging.

Family opinions.

Online "experts."

Everyone has a take. Everyone sounds confident. Most are wrong.

Financial crowd noise creates pressure to act when action is not required. It convinces people that doing nothing is a mistake, when in reality patience is often the correct move.

In wrestling terms, this is reacting to the crowd instead of listening to your corner.

Why Wrestlers Are Especially Vulnerable

Wrestlers are tough. Disciplined. Competitive. Used to suffering.

Those traits are strengths in sport. They can become liabilities with money.

Wrestlers are conditioned to push through pain. Financially, that can lead to ignoring warning signs.

Wrestlers trust effort. Financially, effort alone does not fix bad decisions.

Wrestlers hate losing. Financially, that can lead to doubling down instead of adjusting.

Mental toughness does not mean ignoring reality. It means responding correctly under pressure.

Building Systems for Discipline

The best wrestlers do not rely on emotion.

They rely on systems.

Weight management plans.

Practice schedules.

Recovery routines.

Match strategies.

Money needs the same structure.

Systems protect you when emotions spike.

Examples of financial systems:

- Automatic savings and investing
- Predefined asset allocation
- Clear rules for debt and spending
- Scheduled portfolio reviews

These systems remove decision-making from emotional moments.

In wrestling terms, this is drilling positions until reactions become automatic. You do not think. You execute.

Discipline is not about willpower. It is about design.

Why Willpower Fails Under Stress

Willpower is unreliable.

After a long day.

After a bad loss.

After unexpected expenses.

After market volatility.

Stress drains decision-making capacity. That is when bad choices happen.

Systems exist to protect you when willpower is gone.

A wrestler does not rely on "feeling disciplined" to make weight. They follow a plan. Financial discipline works the same way.

Staying Composed Under Stress

Stress reveals habits.

In wrestling, fatigue reveals technique flaws.

In money, stress reveals planning flaws.

When pressure hits, people default to instinct. If the system is weak, instinct takes over.

Staying composed means:

- Slowing down decisions
- Returning to fundamentals
- Avoiding reactionary moves

You do not win wrestling matches by scrambling emotionally. You win by regaining position.

Financial composure is about staying in position when others panic.

Coach's Perspective

What would your coach say when you start wrestling emotionally?

"Settle down."

"Control the position."

"Don't force it."

"Stay disciplined."

"Next move."

Applied to money:

- Do not panic
- Do not chase
- Do not abandon the plan
- Control what you can control

Coaches do not yell because you are losing. They yell because you are losing composure.

Game Situations and Decision Points

- Markets drop sharply. Do you panic or stick to the plan?
- You see others making money fast. Do you chase or stay disciplined?
- You experience success. Do you increase risk without adjusting protection?

Each moment tests mental discipline more than financial knowledge.

Common Wrestler Mistakes and Financial Parallels

Wrestlers force moves under pressure.

Financially, that is forcing investments.

Wrestlers abandon fundamentals when tired.

Financially, that is abandoning plans during stress.

Wrestlers listen to the crowd instead of the corner.

Financially, that is reacting to noise.

The mistake is not emotion. The mistake is letting emotion drive decisions.

Winning the Long Season

A wrestling career is not defined by one match.

A financial life is not defined by one decision.

The athletes who win long-term are not the most emotional or aggressive. They are the most composed. They stay disciplined through slumps. They trust systems. They respect fundamentals.

Mental control is the edge.

When others panic, you stay steady.

When others chase, you stay patient.

When others react, you execute.

That is how championships are built, on the mat and in life.

Athlete Takeaways

- Fear, greed, and overconfidence are opponents you must manage
- Crowd noise is everywhere, learn to block it out
- Systems protect you when emotions spike
- Discipline beats willpower under stress
- Stay composed, stay in position, and trust the plan

Part V: Life After the Mat

Wrestling does not last forever.

At some point, the practices end, the weigh-ins stop, and the whistle blows for the last time. When that happens, the structure that shaped your daily life disappears quickly. Training schedules, accountability, and clear goals are replaced with open space and new responsibilities.

That transition is where many former wrestlers struggle, not because they lack discipline, but because the system is gone.

Life after the mat brings more decisions than ever before. Career choices, income changes, benefits, housing, and long-term planning all arrive at once. There is no coach setting the calendar and no season telling you when to peak. Money becomes part of every decision, and without structure, it can feel overwhelming.

Wrestling taught you how to control effort, manage pressure, and stay disciplined when it hurts. Those skills still matter. They just need to be applied differently. Budgets replace weight plans. Saving replaces conditioning. Investing replaces long-term development. Planning replaces match strategy.

The mistake is trying to recreate wrestling instead of translating it.

Identity also shifts. For years, being a wrestler defined you. After the mat, success is no longer measured by wins, rankings, or weight classes. It is measured by stability, growth, freedom, and options. The scoreboard changes, but it still matters.

The athletes who thrive after wrestling build new routines on purpose.

They create systems where structure once existed. Automatic habits, scheduled reviews, and clear priorities replace external accountability. Consistency replaces intensity.

Life after the mat is not about losing discipline. It is about choosing where to apply it. The season is longer now, and winning means staying in position, avoiding season-ending mistakes, and stacking good decisions over time.

Key Idea:

The mat may be gone, but the habits that made you successful still win when applied with intention.

Chapter 19: Taxes and Where You Control the Match

Every wrestler understands match control.

You might not score first. You might not be the stronger athlete. But if you control position, pace, and leverage, you stay in the match. You force your opponent to work harder. You limit mistakes. You put yourself in position to win late.

Taxes work the same way.

Most people think taxes are something that just *happen* to them. A number on a paycheck. A line on a return. A surprise bill in April. Wrestlers who succeed financially learn something different. Taxes are not just an outcome. They are a system you can control if you understand positioning.

You may not be able to avoid taxes entirely, but you can absolutely decide *where* the tax pressure shows up and *when* it hits.

That is match control.

Taxable vs Tax-Advantaged Accounts

Not all money is treated the same by the tax system.

A **taxable account** is exactly what it sounds like. You pay taxes as money is earned and again when investments generate income or gains. Checking accounts, savings accounts, and standard brokerage accounts all fall into this category.

A **tax-advantaged account** gives you a rule-based benefit. The government agrees to tax the money differently if you follow specific guidelines. Retirement accounts like 401(k)s, IRAs, and similar plans live here.

In wrestling terms, taxable accounts are neutral position. You can move freely, but you do not get leverage. Tax-advantaged accounts are controlled positions. There are rules, but the leverage is real.

Neither is good or bad on its own. The mistake is not knowing which position you are in.

Many athletes focus only on accessibility. They want money they can touch at any time. That often leads them to overuse taxable accounts and underuse tax-advantaged ones. Convenience feels good in the moment, but it costs control over time.

Understanding the difference lets you choose where each dollar belongs.

Tax-Deferred vs Tax-Free Growth

This is where the leverage really shows up.

Tax-deferred growth means you delay taxes until later. Contributions may reduce taxable income today, but withdrawals are taxed in the future. Traditional retirement accounts work this way.

Tax-free growth means you pay taxes upfront, but qualified withdrawals later are not taxed at all. Roth-style accounts fall into this category.

In wrestling terms, tax-deferred is like conserving energy early. You stay tight, avoid exposure, and plan to score later. Tax-free is like pushing the pace early so the finish is cleaner.

Neither approach is automatically better. The right choice depends on income, career stage, and future expectations.

Young wrestlers early in their careers often have lower incomes. Paying taxes now at a lower rate in exchange for tax-free growth later can be powerful. More established professionals may benefit from deferring taxes when income is high.

The mistake is defaulting without strategy.

If you never think about tax timing, you end up reacting instead of controlling.

Asset Location Basics

Asset allocation gets a lot of attention. Stocks versus bonds. Growth versus stability. That matters, but **asset location** is just as important.

Asset location asks a different question: *Which investments should live in which accounts?*

Some investments generate regular taxable income. Others grow mostly through price appreciation. Placing the wrong investment in the wrong account increases tax drag.

In wrestling terms, this is mat awareness. You do not shoot from the edge the same way you shoot from the center. Position changes strategy.

Examples of smart positioning:

- Tax-efficient growth assets placed in taxable accounts
- Income-producing or frequently traded assets placed in tax-advantaged accounts
- Long-term holdings placed where taxes do the least damage

This is not about perfection. It is about awareness.

Many athletes invest without considering location. Over time, unnecessary taxes quietly bleed performance. The match stays close when it should not be.

Common Tax Mistakes Wrestlers Make

Most tax problems are not dramatic. They are slow pins.

Mistake one: Ignoring taxes completely.

Athletes focus on earning and investing, but never consider tax impact. The result is surprise bills and forced decisions.

Mistake two: Using the wrong account for the wrong goal.

Short-term money locked in retirement accounts. Long-term money sitting fully taxable. Poor positioning creates pressure.

Mistake three: Chasing deductions without a plan.

Deductions feel like wins, but they only matter if they align with long-term strategy. Random moves create complexity, not control.

Mistake four: Forgetting taxes when income changes.

Bonuses, side income, or career shifts can change tax brackets quickly. Wrestlers who do not adjust get caught off balance.

Mistake five: Letting fear drive decisions.

Avoiding taxes entirely leads to avoiding opportunity. Paying attention leads to control. Fear leads to stalling.

None of these mistakes happen in one match. They happen over seasons.

Coach's Perspective

A wrestling coach would keep this simple.

Know the position.

Do not give up leverage.

Think two moves ahead.

Win the small battles.

Stay patient and disciplined.

Taxes are not about trick moves. They are about position and control. Wrestlers who respect that avoid being pinned by surprises.

Game Situations and Decision Points

You earn more money this year.

Do you adjust your tax strategy or keep doing what you did before?

You are choosing where to invest next.

Do you consider taxes, or only returns?

You have money spread across multiple accounts.

Do you know why each dollar is where it is?

These decisions determine who controls the match.

Common Athlete Mistakes and Financial Parallels

Wrestlers force moves from bad position.

Financially, that means ignoring tax impact.

Wrestlers focus only on takedowns.

Financially, that means focusing only on returns.

Wrestlers panic late in matches.

Financially, that means reacting to tax bills instead of planning.

Discipline wins both matches.

Winning the Long Game

Taxes are not an enemy. They are a condition of the sport.

You cannot eliminate them, but you can control exposure. The wrestlers who succeed financially do not avoid taxes. They plan for them, position around them, and use the rules to their advantage.

Match control is not flashy. It is effective.

Athlete Takeaways

- Control position before you try to score
- Know which account you are wrestling from
- Timing matters more than speed
- Poor positioning creates unnecessary pressure
- Discipline over seasons beats scrambling late

Chapter 20: Retirement Accounts and Financial Independence

Every wrestler knows the difference between surviving a match and controlling it.

You can scramble, stall, and fight off attacks just to stay alive, or you can dictate pace, position, and outcome. One approach keeps you exhausted and reactive. The other puts you in command.

That same difference exists in financial life.

Many people approach retirement like survival mode. They hope Social Security is enough. They assume they will "figure it out later." They react to whatever shows up instead of building control early.

Retirement accounts are how you take control of the long match.

Financial independence is not about quitting work early or living on a beach. It is about having options. It is about not being forced into decisions because money pressure is on your neck. It is about being able to choose how hard you wrestle in the later rounds of life.

Employer Plans and Pensions

For many wrestlers turned professionals, the first retirement exposure comes through an employer plan.

These plans include options like 401(k)s, 403(b)s, or similar workplace accounts. The concept is simple. You contribute part of your paycheck. The money is invested. It grows over time.

Some employers offer matching contributions. That is not a bonus. That is compensation. Ignoring a match is like refusing free points.

In wrestling terms, an employer match is your opponent stepping into bad position voluntarily. You do not hesitate. You take it.

Pensions are less common today, but they still exist in certain professions. A pension is a promise of future income, usually based on years of service and salary history. Think of it as a long-term control ride. It rewards consistency and time in the system.

The mistake athletes make is assuming these plans will take care of everything automatically. They will not.

You still choose:

- How much you contribute
- How aggressively the money is invested
- Whether you leave money behind when changing jobs

Employer plans are tools. Tools only work if you use them intentionally.

Traditional and Roth IRAs

Individual Retirement Accounts, or IRAs, give you control outside of an employer system.

A **Traditional IRA** usually allows you to contribute money that may reduce taxable income today. The tradeoff is that withdrawals later are taxed.

A **Roth IRA** flips that structure. You pay taxes now, but qualified withdrawals in the future are tax-free.

In wrestling terms, this is energy management.

Traditional IRAs conserve energy early. You delay the tax hit and deal with it later. Roth IRAs spend energy early so the finish is cleaner.

Neither is automatically better. The right choice depends on income, career stage, and future expectations.

Young wrestlers or early-career professionals often benefit from Roth contributions because income is lower and time is on their side. Established earners may benefit from tax deferral when income peaks.

The real mistake is not choosing wrong. It is not choosing at all.

Many athletes assume retirement accounts are only for later. That belief costs years of compounding. You cannot make up lost mat time.

Contribution Rules and Discipline

Every weight class has limits. Retirement accounts do too.

There are annual contribution limits for employer plans and IRAs. There are income thresholds that affect eligibility. There are penalties for early withdrawals.

These rules are not punishment. They are structure.

In wrestling terms, rules define the match. You do not complain about the mat size. You learn how to wrestle within it.

The most common discipline failures look like this:

- Waiting until the end of the year to contribute
- Contributing inconsistently
- Stopping contributions during minor setbacks
- Pulling money early for convenience

Early withdrawals are especially dangerous. They usually come with taxes, penalties, and lost growth. That is like giving up position voluntarily because you are tired.

Retirement accounts reward consistency. Small, steady contributions matter more than occasional big moves.

This is a conditioning sport, not a sprint.

Retirement Income Basics

Saving money is only half the match. Income is the finish.

Retirement income is about turning accumulated assets into reliable cash flow. That can come from multiple sources:

- Retirement account withdrawals
- Employer plans or pensions
- Social Security
- Investment income

The goal is not to guess how long you will live or predict markets perfectly. The goal is to build enough flexibility that no single source has to carry the entire load.

In wrestling terms, you do not rely on one move to win every match. You chain attacks. You adjust based on position.

Financial independence means:

- You can cover core expenses without stress
- You are not forced to work for survival
- You have margin when life changes

Many athletes misunderstand retirement because they think of it as an age. It is not.

It is a position.

When your money can support your life choices, you are independent regardless of age.

Why Wrestlers Struggle With Retirement Planning

Wrestlers are used to short time horizons.

Seasons are short. Matches are intense. Weight cuts are immediate. The future feels distant compared to the grind in front of you.

That mindset creates problems financially.

Retirement rewards:

- Patience
- Long-term thinking
- Consistent effort without visible results

Those are skills wrestlers already have, but they are rarely applied to money.

Another issue is identity. Wrestlers pride themselves on toughness and self-reliance. Asking for help or planning for vulnerability later can feel uncomfortable.

Ignoring retirement planning does not make you tough. It makes you exposed.

Coach's Perspective

A wrestling coach would not overcomplicate this.

Show up every day.

Make weight consistently.

Do not give away points.

Stay in position.

Finish strong.

Retirement accounts are not exciting. They are effective. Coaches do not care if conditioning is fun. They care if it works.

Game Situations and Decision Points

You change jobs.

Do you roll your retirement account forward or cash it out?

You get a raise.

Do you increase contributions or inflate lifestyle?

You feel behind.

Do you panic and force decisions, or recommit to consistency?

These are match moments. Awareness matters.

Common Athlete Mistakes and Financial Parallels

Wrestlers cut corners on conditioning.

Financially, that means skipping contributions.

Wrestlers focus only on takedowns.

Financially, that means saving without planning income.

Wrestlers panic late in matches.

Financially, that means reacting emotionally to markets.

The same discipline that wins matches builds independence.

Winning the Long Game

Retirement is not one match. It is a career.

You do not need perfection. You need consistency. Wrestlers who build financial independence do not rely on luck. They rely on reps, rules, and patience.

Control position early. Stay disciplined. Finish on your terms.

Athlete Takeaways

- Retirement accounts are about control, not age
- Employer matches are free points. Take them
- Roth and Traditional accounts are timing tools
- Consistency beats intensity over decades
- Financial independence is position, not retirement age

Chapter 21: Housing and Big Financial Decisions

Every wrestler remembers the first time they tried to force a move that was not there.

Maybe you shot when your opponent was perfectly squared. Maybe you went for a throw without setting it up. For a moment it felt aggressive and confident. Seconds later, you were on your back wondering how it went wrong so fast.

Big financial decisions work the same way.

Housing, cars, and major purchases are not just expenses. They are commitments that affect your balance, flexibility, and ability to compete over the long haul. When they fit your position, they strengthen your base. When they are forced, they put you in danger every round that follows.

This chapter is about learning when to shoot, when to circle, and when to stay in position.

Renting vs Buying: Position Before Pressure

In wrestling, position comes before offense.

If your stance is off or your balance is compromised, even the best move fails. Housing decisions are no different.

Renting provides flexibility. Buying provides stability and potential long-term upside. Neither is automatically good or bad. The mistake is treating buying like a trophy instead of a strategic decision.

Renting is like staying light on your feet.

You can move for work.

You are not responsible for repairs.

You can adjust quickly if income changes.

For early-career wrestlers or athletes transitioning into the workforce, renting often protects flexibility. Flexibility matters when you are still figuring out weight class, career direction, and income stability.

Buying is like committing to a position.

You build equity over time.

You control your environment.

You lock in housing costs in many cases.

Buying makes sense when income is stable, location is clear, and you are ready to handle responsibility. Buying too early is like tying up in a bad position and hoping strength saves you.

The real question is not "Can I buy?"

It is "Does buying fit my position right now?"

Mortgages and Down Payments: Understanding the Hold

A mortgage is leverage.

It allows you to control an expensive asset with borrowed money. Leverage can help you win. It can also magnify mistakes.

In wrestling terms, a mortgage is a tight hold. When you understand it, you can control the match. When you do not, you burn energy trying to escape your own decision.

Down payments matter because they determine leverage.

A larger down payment lowers monthly payments and reduces risk.

A smaller down payment increases flexibility upfront but raises long-term pressure.

There is no universal right answer. What matters is margin.

Too many athletes stretch into homes that consume too much income. That leaves no room for:

- Career changes
- Unexpected expenses
- Savings or investing

That is wrestling with your back near the edge of the mat every day.

A home should support your life, not dominate it.

Cars, Leases, and Financing Traps

Cars are one of the fastest ways athletes give away position.

Transportation is necessary. Overpaying for it is optional.

Car purchases often come with:

- Long loan terms
- High interest rates
- Rapid depreciation

In wrestling terms, buying too much car is like carrying extra weight into a match. You can still compete, but everything feels harder.

Leases look attractive because payments are lower. The tradeoff is control. You never own the asset. You are locked into rules, mileage limits, and ongoing payments.

Leasing can make sense in very specific situations. For most athletes, it becomes a cycle of permanent payments with no long-term value.

Financing traps show up when:

- Payments feel affordable but total cost is ignored
- Loan terms stretch to six or seven years
- Lifestyle upgrades happen faster than income growth

Cars should get you to work and training. They should not consume future options.

Planning Major Purchases Like a Match

Wrestlers plan matches. They do not freestyle for seven minutes.

Big financial decisions deserve the same respect.

Before committing to housing, vehicles, or large purchases, ask:

- What does this cost monthly and long-term?
- How does this affect savings and investing?
- What happens if income changes?
- Does this improve my position or limit it?

Most mistakes happen when decisions are made emotionally. Excitement. Comparison. Pressure from peers. Fear of missing out.

That is crowd noise talking.

Smart wrestlers slow the match down. They feel the pressure and respond with discipline.

Why Athletes Feel Pressure to "Upgrade"

Athletes are competitive by nature. That does not stop after sports.

Titles, houses, cars, and lifestyle become the new scoreboard. Social media amplifies this pressure. It looks like everyone else is winning.

But comparison is a bad opponent.

Buying a house too early or financing a lifestyle to look successful creates stress that shows up years later. Wrestlers know that bad weight cuts do not always hurt immediately. The damage shows up in later matches.

The same is true financially.

Coach's Perspective

A wrestling coach would be blunt.

Stay in position.

Do not force it.

Make them move first.

Win the long match.

Do not give away easy points.

Housing and big purchases should be boring decisions executed well. Coaches do not praise flashy decisions that lose matches.

Match Situations and Decision Points

You qualify for a bigger mortgage.

Do you take the maximum or choose margin?

You want a new car after a good year.

Do you buy momentum or protect flexibility?

Friends are buying homes.

Do you follow them or follow your position?

These decisions decide matches long after the first whistle.

Common Athlete Mistakes and Financial Parallels

Wrestlers force shots.

Financially, that means rushing big purchases.

Wrestlers chase points early.

Financially, that means upgrading lifestyle too fast.

Wrestlers ignore position.

Financially, that means ignoring cash flow and margin.

Discipline prevents pins.

Winning the Long Game

Housing and major purchases are not about status. They are about sustainability.

The wrestlers who win long careers understand patience. They wait for position. They choose control over flash. They protect their base so they can attack when it matters.

Financial independence is built the same way.

Stay balanced. Stay flexible. Make moves that keep you on your feet.

Athlete Takeaways

- Renting and buying are position decisions, not status symbols
- Mortgages are leverage. Respect the hold
- Cars should support life, not restrict it
- Big purchases deserve match-level planning
- Control position now so you can finish later

Chapter 22: Your Career Is Your Training Plan

Every wrestler understands this truth early.

You do not just show up on match day and hope things work out. You follow a training plan. Lifts are scheduled. Conditioning is programmed. Technique is drilled. Recovery is managed. Weight is monitored. Everything you do outside the match determines what happens when the whistle blows.

Your career works the same way.

Income does not happen by accident. Stability does not happen by accident. Long-term success is not luck. It is the result of decisions made consistently over time, often when no one is watching.

Your career is your training plan for your financial life.

If you approach it casually, you get casual results. If you approach it with discipline, intention, and awareness, you build momentum that compounds year after year.

Salary vs Total Compensation: Know the Full Scorecard

Many athletes fixate on one number: salary.

That is like focusing only on takedowns and ignoring riding time, escapes, and near-fall. You might think you are winning while the scoreboard tells a different story.

Salary is just the base pay.

Total compensation includes everything else:

- Bonuses
- Retirement contributions
- Health insurance
- Disability coverage
- Paid time off
- Stock options or profit sharing
- Education benefits

In wrestling terms, salary is your hand fighting. Total compensation is the entire match.

A job with a lower salary but strong benefits can put you in a much better long-term position than a higher salary with no support. Health insurance alone can be worth thousands per year. Employer retirement matches are literally free points if you take advantage of them.

Athletes who ignore benefits are leaving points on the mat.

Before accepting or leaving a job, ask:

- What is the full compensation package?
- What am I responsible for paying myself?
- How does this affect my long-term financial conditioning?

You would never cut weight without knowing the scale. Do not accept compensation without knowing the full picture.

Job Changes and Benefits: Transitioning Without Losing Position

Wrestlers know transitions are dangerous.

Scrambles. Mat returns. Neutral resets. One bad transition can undo a full period of work.

Career changes work the same way.

Changing jobs can increase income, expand skills, and create opportunity.

It can also expose gaps if you are not paying attention.

Common transition mistakes include:

- Forgetting to roll over retirement accounts
- Losing health coverage temporarily
- Not understanding vesting schedules
- Accepting higher pay with weaker benefits

Every job change should be treated like a match transition.

Before you move, understand:

- When benefits start and end
- What happens to retirement accounts
- Whether insurance coverage overlaps
- How income timing changes

Smart wrestlers reset position before attacking again. Smart professionals secure benefits and systems before chasing the next opportunity.

Negotiation Basics: Competing Without Emotion

Negotiation makes athletes uncomfortable.

That surprises people, but it makes sense. Wrestlers are taught to let performance speak. Grind harder. Outwork everyone. Do not ask. Earn it.

Negotiation is not begging. It is competition.

In wrestling terms, negotiation is hand fighting. You establish position, create angles, and apply pressure without losing balance.

Good negotiation is built on:

- Preparation
- Data
- Calm confidence
- Willingness to walk away

You do not threaten. You do not bluff recklessly. You communicate value.

Key principles athletes should remember:

- Everything is negotiable at the beginning
- It is harder to renegotiate later
- Silence is a tool
- The worst they can say is no

Negotiating salary, benefits, flexibility, or role is not selfish. It is professional. Coaches negotiate schedules, travel, and resources all the time. You are allowed to advocate for yourself.

Just like wrestling, negotiation rewards those who stay composed and do not force moves.

Side Income and Entrepreneurship: Extra Conditioning, Not Chaos

Many wrestlers train outside official practice.

Extra lifts. Extra drilling. Extra conditioning. Done correctly, it sharpens performance. Done poorly, it leads to burnout or injury.

Side income works the same way.

Side businesses, consulting, coaching, content creation, or entrepreneurship can:

- Increase income
- Build skills
- Create flexibility
- Reduce reliance on one employer

They can also:

- Drain time and focus
- Create tax complications
- Increase stress

- Distract from primary performance

Side income should support your career, not sabotage it.

Ask yourself:

- Does this align with my long-term goals?
- Does it improve skills or just chase money?
- Do I understand the tax implications?
- Can I sustain this without burning out?

In wrestling terms, side income should feel like smart supplemental conditioning, not weight-cut panic cardio the night before weigh-ins.

Why Athletes Struggle With Career Patience

Athletes are used to clear progression.

Freshman to starter. Varsity to conference. Conference to national level. The path is structured.

Careers are not.

Progress is uneven. Feedback is unclear. Politics exist. Performance is not always rewarded immediately. That frustrates former athletes who are used to clear scoreboards.

This leads to:

- Job hopping too fast
- Chasing titles instead of development
- Leaving before skills fully compound

Wrestlers know that mastery takes time. Moves that feel awkward early become automatic after years of reps.

Careers are the same. Early years are about skill accumulation, not dominance. Patience is part of the plan.

Coach's Perspective

A wrestling coach would be direct.

Trust the process.

Reps matter.

Stay disciplined.

Do not cut corners.

Build your base before you chase points.

Careers are not won in one season. They are built through consistent preparation.

Match Situations and Decision Points

You get a job offer with higher pay but weaker benefits.

Do you chase points or protect position?

You feel underpaid.

Do you negotiate with preparation or quit emotionally?

You want a side hustle.

Do you add smart conditioning or overload yourself?

These are match decisions. Awareness wins.

Common Athlete Mistakes and Financial Parallels

Wrestlers chase quick pins.

Financially, that means chasing titles over skills.

Wrestlers ignore conditioning.

Financially, that means ignoring benefits and systems.

Wrestlers panic in scrambles.

Financially, that means job hopping without a plan.

Discipline keeps you in control.

Winning the Long Game

Your career is not separate from your finances. It is the engine that funds everything else.

Wrestlers who succeed long-term understand that training never really stops. They adjust. They recover. They refine. They stay patient.

The same approach builds financial independence.

Do not rush the process. Build skills. Negotiate smart. Protect benefits. Add income intentionally. Let your career compound.

Athlete Takeaways

- Salary is only part of the score. Know total compensation
- Job changes are transitions. Secure position before moving
- Negotiation is competition, not confrontation
- Side income should support your base, not break it
- Treat your career like a long-term training plan

Chapter 23: Estate Planning Basics Everyone Needs

Every wrestler has been in this position.

You are winning the match. You control the center. Your opponent is reacting. Then, late in the period, you make one small mistake. A bad reach. A loose tie. You get caught, and suddenly everything changes. All the work you put in is undone because you failed to protect position at the right moment.

Estate planning works the same way.

You can work your entire life building income, saving money, investing wisely, and staying disciplined, but without basic estate planning, one unexpected event can unravel everything. Estate planning is not about being old, wealthy, or pessimistic. It is about protecting position when you are not able to fight for it yourself.

In wrestling terms, estate planning is match awareness when you are exhausted, injured, or off the mat entirely. It ensures your effort still counts.

Why Estate Planning Is Not Optional

Most athletes avoid estate planning for one simple reason. It feels uncomfortable.

Talking about death, incapacity, or emergencies feels like inviting bad outcomes. Wrestlers are wired to focus on control, toughness, and resilience. Planning for things you cannot control feels wrong.

But wrestling teaches the opposite lesson.

You prepare for worst-case scenarios so they do not beat you.

You drill defense not because you expect to be taken down, but because you know it can happen. Estate planning is that same defensive preparation.

Without it:

- Courts decide what happens to your assets
- Family members may fight or get confused
- Money can be delayed, misused, or lost
- Medical decisions may be made by people you would not choose

Estate planning is not about predicting the future. It is about reducing chaos when pressure hits.

Wills: Setting the Basic Game Plan

A will is the foundation.

It is a legal document that states what happens to your assets when you pass away and who is responsible for carrying out your wishes. It also allows you to name guardians for minor children.

In wrestling terms, a will is your match strategy written down.

Without a will, the state creates one for you. That is like letting your opponent choose your game plan. The outcome may not reflect your values, priorities, or intentions.

A will allows you to:

- Decide who receives what
- Name an executor to handle logistics
- Name guardians for children
- Reduce confusion and delays

Common athlete mistake: thinking a will is only needed if you have a lot of money.

That is wrong.

If you have:

- A bank account
- A vehicle
- Personal property
- Children
- Debt

You need a will.

A simple plan beats no plan every time.

Trusts: Control, Efficiency, and Flexibility

Trusts add structure.

A trust is a legal arrangement that holds assets and distributes them according to rules you set. Trusts can be used during life, after death, or both.

In wrestling terms, a trust is superior position. It gives you control and limits your opponent's options.

Trusts can:

- Avoid probate delays
- Provide privacy
- Control how and when money is distributed
- Protect beneficiaries from poor decisions or creditors
- Manage assets if you become incapacitated

Trusts are not just for the ultra-wealthy. They are tools.

For athletes and former athletes, trusts often make sense when:

- You have children
- You want to control timing of distributions

- You want to protect assets long-term
- You have complex family situations

A trust does not replace a will. It works alongside it.

Just like wrestling, layers of defense matter.

Beneficiaries and Account Titling: The Details That Decide Matches

This is where many plans fail.

Beneficiaries and account titling determine who receives assets like:

- Retirement accounts
- Life insurance
- Investment accounts
- Bank accounts

These designations override your will.

In wrestling terms, this is hand position. Small details that decide outcomes.

If your beneficiaries are outdated, incorrect, or missing, assets may:

- Go to the wrong person
- Be delayed
- Create legal disputes
- Trigger unnecessary taxes

Common athlete mistakes:

- Never updating beneficiaries after marriage or divorce
- Naming minors directly
- Forgetting about old accounts
- Assuming a will fixes everything

Estate planning is not set-it-and-forget-it. It requires periodic review, especially after life changes.

Details win matches. Details protect families.

Powers of Attorney: Control When You Cannot Compete

A power of attorney allows someone you trust to make decisions on your behalf if you are unable to do so.

There are two main types:

- Financial power of attorney
- Medical power of attorney

In wrestling terms, this is having a trusted coach make decisions when you are injured.

Without powers of attorney:

- Bills may go unpaid
- Accounts may be frozen
- Medical decisions may be delayed
- Courts may step in

A power of attorney allows someone to:

- Pay bills
- Manage accounts
- Make medical decisions
- Handle legal matters

This is not about giving up control. It is about choosing who steps in if you cannot act.

Every wrestler understands the importance of a corner you trust. Powers of attorney are that corner.

Healthcare Directives: Your Voice Under Pressure

A healthcare directive, often called a living will, outlines your wishes for medical care if you cannot communicate them yourself.

It answers questions like:

- What treatments do you want or not want?
- Who speaks for you?
- How aggressive should care be?

In wrestling terms, this is pre-planned strategy for injury scenarios.

Without a healthcare directive:

- Family members may disagree
- Doctors may make assumptions
- Decisions may not reflect your values

These documents reduce emotional burden on loved ones. They give clarity when clarity matters most.

Strong wrestlers plan for exhaustion. Strong families plan for emergencies.

Why Athletes Delay Estate Planning

Athletes delay estate planning for predictable reasons:

- "I am too young"
- "I do not have enough money"
- "Nothing will happen"
- "I will do it later"

Wrestlers know better.

Later is not a plan. Later is how matches are lost.

Estate planning is not about age. It is about responsibility. If someone else would be affected by your absence, you need a plan.

Coach's Perspective

A wrestling coach would be blunt.

Protect position.

Handle your business.

Details matter.

Do not leave things to chance.

Finish the match the right way.

Estate planning is not emotional. It is disciplined.

Match Situations and Decision Points

You have children but no will.

Do you protect them or hope nothing happens?

You have retirement accounts with outdated beneficiaries.

Do you assume it is fine or fix it?

You trust someone to help if you are injured.

Have you given them legal authority?

These are match decisions. Avoiding them does not stop the clock.

Common Athlete Mistakes and Financial Parallels

Wrestlers ignore defense until it costs them.

Financially, that means ignoring estate planning.

Wrestlers lose matches on details.

Financially, that means bad beneficiary designations.

Wrestlers wait too long to adjust.

Financially, that means planning after a crisis.

Preparation beats regret.

Winning the Long Game

Estate planning is about respect.

Respect for your work.

Respect for your family.

Respect for the people who would have to clean up the mess.

Wrestlers understand finishing strong. Estate planning is finishing strong for life.

You do not need perfection. You need a plan.

Athlete Takeaways

- A will is your basic game plan. Do not let the state choose for you
- Trusts add control and structure when situations get complex
- Beneficiaries and titling are small details that decide outcomes
- Powers of attorney protect you when you cannot compete
- Estate planning is defense. Protect position even when you are off the mat

Chapter 24: Talking About Money With Family

Every wrestler knows this feeling.

You step into the practice room and everything makes sense. The rules are clear. The goals are defined. The work is hard, but straightforward. Then you step outside the room and things get messy. Emotions. Expectations. Unspoken rules. Conflicting agendas.

Talking about money with family feels like that.

It is rarely about numbers alone. It is about roles, history, power, fear, and identity. For wrestlers who grew up in structured environments, this shift can be jarring. You are used to clear authority, clear feedback, and clear consequences. Family money conversations rarely offer any of that.

But just like wrestling, avoiding the hard conversations does not make the match easier. It makes it harder later.

Why Money and Family Collide

Money is emotional because it represents security, freedom, sacrifice, and control.

Family is emotional because it carries history, expectations, and unspoken contracts.

When those two meet, logic often loses.

Wrestlers are trained to separate emotion from execution. You cannot afford to wrestle angry, scared, or distracted. Money conversations with family require the same discipline.

If you do not address money openly:

- Assumptions fill the gap
- Resentment builds quietly
- Boundaries blur
- Decisions get made under pressure instead of planning

In wrestling terms, this is giving up position early and hoping you can scramble out later.

Teaching Kids About Money: Building Fundamentals Early

Wrestlers understand this better than anyone.

You do not wait until someone is varsity to teach stance and motion. You start early. Reps matter.

Money education for kids works the same way.

Teaching kids about money is not about spreadsheets or investing jargon. It is about habits, values, and awareness.

Core lessons kids need:

- Money is earned
- Money is finite
- Money involves choices
- Money reflects priorities

In wrestling terms, this is drilling basics.

Allowance, chores, saving jars, and simple conversations about spending are the equivalent of learning to sprawl and hand fight. They build muscle memory.

Common athlete-parent mistake: shielding kids completely from money.

The intention is protection. The result is ignorance.

Kids who never see money decisions grow up unprepared. Just like wrestlers who never see live competition struggle when it matters.

Age-appropriate transparency builds confidence, not anxiety.

College and Young Adults: Letting Them Wrestle Their Own Matches

This is one of the hardest transitions for parents and former athletes.

You are used to structure. You want to help. You see mistakes coming before they happen.

But development requires experience.

College and early adulthood are like a wrestler's first seasons at a higher level. They will get exposed. They will make mistakes. That is part of growth.

Money conversations with young adults should shift from control to guidance.

Instead of:

- "Do this"
- "Do not do that"

The conversation becomes:

- "Here is how to think about this"
- "Here are the consequences"
- "Here is how I would approach it"

In wrestling terms, this is moving from coach to corner. You are not on the mat anymore, but your voice still matters.

Key money topics for this stage:

- Budgeting with real income
- Credit cards and debt
- Student loans

- Rent and basic living costs
- Saving before lifestyle upgrades

The mistake many families make is rescuing too quickly.

Constant financial bailouts prevent learning. Wrestlers who never feel the consequence of bad positioning never fix it.

Support growth, not dependence.

Aging Parents and Caregiving: A New Weight Class

This is where roles truly reverse.

One day you realize the people who taught you discipline, sacrifice, and resilience may need your help. Financially. Logistically. Emotionally.

This transition is heavy.

Money conversations with aging parents are difficult because they challenge identity. Parents are used to providing. Accepting help can feel like weakness.

Wrestlers understand weight classes. You adjust your strategy based on reality, not ego.

These conversations should focus on:

- Safety
- Sustainability
- Dignity
- Shared planning

Important topics include:

- Income sources
- Healthcare costs
- Insurance coverage
- Housing plans
- Legal documents

- Long-term care wishes

The biggest mistake is waiting until a crisis.

Emergency conversations lead to rushed decisions, stress, and conflict. Planning conversations create clarity and control.

In wrestling terms, this is preparing for overtime before the match goes there.

Family Expectations: The Invisible Pressure

Many former athletes feel this deeply.

You were the disciplined one. The hard worker. The one who "made it." That identity can quietly turn into financial expectation.

Sometimes it is explicit. Sometimes it is unspoken.

Family expectations can include:

- Helping siblings
- Supporting parents
- Paying for group expenses
- Being the financial safety net

None of these are automatically wrong. The problem is when expectations are assumed rather than discussed.

Wrestlers know that unspoken rules create chaos. You need clarity.

You are allowed to care without overextending. You are allowed to help without sacrificing your future. You are allowed to say no without guilt.

Boundaries are not selfish. They are structure.

Setting Boundaries Without Burning Bridges

This is where many athletes struggle.

You are used to pushing through discomfort. You are used to sacrificing. You are used to putting the team first.

Money boundaries feel like quitting.

They are not.

In wrestling terms, boundaries are position. They keep you from being controlled.

Healthy boundaries sound like:

- "I can help in this way, but not that way"
- "I am not able to do that financially"
- "I need to protect my long-term goals"
- "Let's talk about a plan instead of reacting"

Boundaries should be:

- Clear
- Calm
- Consistent

You do not need to justify every decision. Over-explaining invites debate. State your position and hold it.

Just like on the mat, hesitation creates openings.

Coach's Perspective

A wrestling coach would be direct.

Control what you can control.

Protect position.

Do not wrestle emotionally.

Have a plan before the whistle.

Respect yourself and the people around you.

Money conversations are not about winning arguments. They are about maintaining control and long-term stability.

Match Situations and Decision Points

Your child wants financial help but avoids responsibility.

Do you rescue or teach?

A parent avoids discussing finances.

Do you push gently now or wait for a crisis?

Family members expect support.

Do you assume responsibility or define limits?

These are not one-time decisions. They are ongoing matches.

Common Athlete Mistakes and Financial Parallels

Wrestlers try to muscle through bad position.

Financially, that means absorbing family pressure without boundaries.

Wrestlers avoid uncomfortable training.

Financially, that means avoiding hard conversations.

Wrestlers fight emotionally.

Financially, that leads to reactive decisions and regret.

Discipline applies off the mat too.

Winning the Long Game

Talking about money with family is not about perfection. It is about consistency, clarity, and respect.

Strong families are not those without conflict. They are those willing to address it early, calmly, and honestly.

Wrestlers understand that preparation reduces panic. These conversations are part of preparation.

You are not responsible for everyone's outcomes. You are responsible for how you show up, how you communicate, and how you protect your future.

That is leadership.

Athlete Takeaways

- Teach money fundamentals early, just like stance and motion
- Shift from control to guidance as kids grow
- Address aging-parent finances before emergencies force decisions
- Set clear boundaries to protect position and relationships
- Calm, disciplined conversations beat emotional reactions every time

Part VI: Winning the Long Season

Wrestling seasons are not won in one match.

They are won in early mornings, long practices, weight cuts done the right way, and the discipline to show up when motivation is gone. Anyone who has wrestled understands this truth. The grind is constant. The spotlight is rare. The results only show up for those who stay committed long after others fade.

Money works the same way.

There is no single decision that guarantees financial success. There is no perfect investment, job, or shortcut that replaces consistency. Winning financially is about surviving bad periods, staying disciplined during good ones, and continuing to execute when the outcome is uncertain.

The long season is where most people lose focus.

Early success creates overconfidence. Setbacks create doubt. Life distractions pull attention away. Without systems, discipline erodes quietly. Just like in wrestling, the opponent is not always across from you. Often, it is fatigue, impatience, and complacency.

This final section is about staying grounded.

It is about understanding when to ask for help, how to protect yourself from bad actors, and how to keep your financial fundamentals intact over decades, not months. It is about recognizing that smart decisions compound, while small mistakes repeated over time quietly undermine progress.

Wrestlers are uniquely prepared for this reality.

You already know how to:

- Train when results are delayed
- Follow a plan through adversity
- Trust preparation over emotion
- Respect process over hype

Those same traits win financially.

Part VI is not about learning something new. It is about reinforcing what matters most when pressure increases and time stretches on. It is about protecting the work you have already done and continuing to show up with discipline, even when no one is watching.

The season is long.

The athletes who win are not the most talented. They are the most consistent.

Chapter 25: Advisors, Scams, and Long-Term Success

Every great basketball player knows this truth.

You do not win alone.

No matter how talented you are, you rely on coaches, trainers, teammates, scouts, film coordinators, and medical staff. Even the best players in the world have people around them helping with preparation, strategy, and decision-making.

Money works the same way.

Trying to manage everything yourself forever is not strength. It is isolation. Knowing when to get help, who to trust, and how to avoid bad advice is what separates athletes who build long-term stability from those who keep starting over.

This chapter is about learning when to pass the ball, how to recognize traps, and how to play the long game without beating yourself.

When to Seek Professional Help

Athletes are trained to be self-reliant.

You push through fatigue. You fight through pressure. You are rewarded for toughness. That mindset helps you compete. Financially, it can hurt you.

There are moments when getting help is not weakness. It is awareness.

You should consider professional help when:

Your income becomes inconsistent or complex

You have multiple sources of income

You are dealing with taxes, contracts, or NIL money

You are transitioning careers

You are managing debt, investing, or planning long-term

You feel overwhelmed or unsure

In basketball terms, this is recognizing when the game has sped up.

Early on, you can rely on instinct. As the competition increases, instinct alone is not enough. You need scouting reports. Film breakdown. Game planning.

Money reaches the same point.

If decisions feel confusing, stressful, or too important to guess on, that is your signal. You do not wait until you are losing badly to call a timeout.

Types of Financial Advisors and What They Do

Not all advisors do the same job.

This is where athletes get confused. Someone says they are a financial advisor, but that title can mean very different things. Understanding roles helps you avoid mismatches.

Fiduciary Advisors

A fiduciary is legally required to act in your best interest.

They are paid to give advice, not to sell products. This is the closest comparison to a head coach. Their job is to help you make decisions that fit your long-term goals, not just win one possession.

They focus on planning, strategy, and alignment.

Commission-Based Advisors

These advisors earn money by selling financial products.

This does not automatically make them bad, but it creates conflicts. Their incentives matter. This is like a coach who gets paid more for calling certain plays, regardless of whether they fit the team.

You must understand how they are compensated before trusting advice.

Accountants and Tax Professionals

Accountants focus on compliance and tax strategy.

They help you understand what you owe, what you can deduct, and how decisions affect your tax situation. In basketball terms, they are the film room specialists. They make sure details are correct.

They are essential, but they do not usually help with overall strategy.

Attorneys

Attorneys help with legal structure, contracts, and protection.

They are critical for athletes dealing with NIL, businesses, estate planning, or liability. In basketball terms, they are the rule experts. They help you avoid violations that can cost you later.

No single professional does everything. Great outcomes come from the right team, not one hero.

Recognizing Scams and Bad Advice

This is where many athletes get hurt.

Scams target confidence, not ignorance. They sound good because they are designed to.

Red flags include:

Guaranteed returns

Pressure to act quickly

Secret or exclusive opportunities

Complex explanations that avoid clear answers

Dismissal of questions

Statements like "everyone is doing this"

In basketball terms, this is someone calling for a wild shot early in the clock with no spacing and no backup plan.

If you do not understand how something works, that is not your failure. That is your warning sign.

Real opportunities can be explained clearly. Scams rely on urgency and confusion.

Why Athletes Are Targeted

Athletes are visible.

You are perceived as having income, potential, or future earnings. That attracts people with bad intentions. Some will be obvious. Others will look like helpers.

The most dangerous advice often comes from people who sound confident but are unqualified.

Locker room advice spreads fast. Someone made money once. Someone knows someone. Stories get exaggerated. Details get lost.

Basketball punishes freelancing. Money does too.

Ten Common Financial Mistakes Athletes Make

1. **Confusing income with wealth**
2. High income does not mean stability.
3. **Skipping saving early**
4. Protection comes before growth.
5. **Taking on lifestyle debt**
6. Comfort now creates pressure later.
7. **Chasing hot investments**
8. Highlights are not a strategy.
9. **Ignoring taxes**
10. They do not go away.
11. **Trusting the wrong people**
12. Proximity does not equal expertise.
13. **Avoiding uncomfortable numbers**

14. Avoidance increases damage.
15. **Waiting too long to get help**
16. Early guidance saves years.
17. **Overestimating future income**
18. Nothing is guaranteed.
19. **Changing plans emotionally**
20. Discipline beats reaction.

These mistakes are not about intelligence. They are about lack of structure.

Ten Rules for Long-Term Financial Success

1. **Know the score at all times**
2. Track income, spending, and net worth.
3. **Protect yourself first**
4. Emergency funds and insurance matter.
5. **Live below your means**
6. Margin creates freedom.
7. **Automate good behavior**
8. Remove emotion from saving and investing.
9. **Understand before you act**
10. Never invest in what you cannot explain.
11. **Build a team, not a dependency**
12. You should understand your plan.
13. **Avoid urgency**
14. Good decisions survive time.
15. **Focus on consistency, not perfection**
16. Small wins compound.
17. **Review and adjust**
18. Plans evolve as life changes.
19. **Play the long game**
20. Longevity beats flash.

These rules are boring for the same reason fundamentals are boring. They work.

Coach's Perspective

A coach would say it clearly.

Trust the system.

Ask for help early.

Protect yourself from turnovers.

Stay disciplined.

Great teams do not rely on talent alone. They rely on preparation and structure.

Money rewards the same approach.

Game Situations and Decision Points

You feel overwhelmed. Do you ask for help or guess?

You hear about a big opportunity. Do you slow down or rush in?

Someone gives advice. Do you check credentials or trust confidence?

Just like basketball, awareness decides outcomes.

Winning the Long Game

Basketball careers are short.

Financial lives are long.

The goal is not to win every possession. The goal is to stay in the game long enough for discipline to matter. Athletes who succeed long after the final buzzer are not the ones who chased shortcuts. They are the ones who respected fundamentals, built teams, avoided traps, and stayed patient.

That is how you finish strong.

Athlete Takeaways

Seek help when the game speeds up

Understand who you are listening to

Avoid guarantees and pressure

Learn from common mistakes

Play for longevity, not highlights

The smartest play is not always the flashiest one.

Sometimes, it is the pass that keeps the offense running and the game under control.

Chapter 26: Losing the Schedule and Rebuilding Structure

One of the hardest adjustments after sports has nothing to do with money, work, or even identity.

It is the schedule.

For most of your life as an athlete, someone else controlled your time. Wake-up times. Lift times. Practice windows. Film sessions. Travel schedules. Meals. Meetings. Curfews. Even rest was planned for you.

You did not have to decide when to train. You were told.

You did not have to decide when to recover. It was built in.

You did not have to decide what mattered most that day. The schedule decided for you.

Then one day, the schedule disappears.

No practice.

No lifts.

No meetings.

No season calendar on the wall.

Just open time.

And open time sounds like freedom until you realize how much structure you lost without noticing.

Why Life Gets Harder When No One Is Setting Your Calendar

Athletes are often described as disciplined. And that is true, but only part of the story.

What athletes are really good at is **executing within structure**.

You show up on time.

You follow the plan.

You do the work.

You repeat.

That discipline was reinforced every single day by external systems. Coaches. Trainers. Academic advisors. Team rules. Consequences.

When those systems disappear, discipline becomes optional.

Not intentionally. Quietly.

There is no whistle when you skip a workout.

No coach calling you out for missing film.

No teammate holding you accountable for sleeping in.

And because nothing immediately breaks, it feels harmless.

That is how habits erode.

Financial habits are often the first thing to suffer because they rely heavily on consistency and delayed reward. Missing one savings transfer does not feel like missing practice. Skipping a budget check does not feel like missing a lift.

But over time, the effects compound.

Structure does not disappear loudly.

It fades quietly.

From Mandatory Workouts to Optional Discipline

In sports, discipline is enforced.

You do not debate whether to show up. You show up.

You do not negotiate intensity. You match the standard.

You do not skip reps because you are tired. You modify, but you still train.

After sports, discipline becomes a choice.

You choose when to wake up.

You choose whether to work out.

You choose whether to review finances.

You choose whether to plan or react.

That shift is harder than most people expect.

Optional discipline feels lighter, but it is weaker. It relies on motivation, and motivation is inconsistent. Stress, fatigue, social pressure, and distraction all chip away at it.

This is why many former athletes say things like:

"I don't know why this feels harder than playing."

It feels harder because you are now responsible for **creating the structure that used to be given to you**.

And without structure, even disciplined people drift.

How Lack of Structure Quietly Breaks Financial Habits

Financial breakdowns rarely come from one big mistake.

They come from **missed reps**.

Not checking accounts.

Not tracking spending.

Not saving automatically.

Not reviewing debt.

Not planning ahead.

None of these feel urgent in the moment.

Bills still get paid.

Money still comes in.

Life keeps moving.

But over time, the absence of structure creates friction.

You stop saving consistently.

Spending becomes reactive.

Decisions are made based on convenience instead of intention.

Stress increases because nothing feels under control.

This is not a willpower problem.

It is a systems problem.

Athletes understand this better than most. You would never rely on "feeling motivated" to stay in shape during the season. You rely on schedules, accountability, and routines.

Money requires the same approach.

When the schedule disappears, the habits disappear with it unless you replace them deliberately.

Why "I'll Do It Later" Is the New Enemy

In sports, later rarely exists.

You lift when it is scheduled.

You practice when it is scheduled.

You prepare when it is scheduled.

After sports, everything becomes flexible.

"I'll look at my finances later."

"I'll start saving when things settle down."

"I'll plan once I make more money."

Later becomes permanent.

This is dangerous because financial progress depends more on **timing and consistency** than intensity. Small actions done regularly matter more than big actions done occasionally.

The longer structure is missing, the harder it is to rebuild.

That is why many former athletes feel behind financially even when they are working hard. Effort without structure leaks.

Replacing Practice Schedules With Personal Systems

The solution is not motivation.

It is **replacement**.

You do not need to recreate your old schedule.

You need to replace its function.

A practice schedule did a few key things:

It told you **when** to act.

It removed decision-making.

It created repetition.

It built accountability.

It protected progress during low-motivation days.

Your financial system needs to do the same.

This starts with time-based structure, not complexity.

Set specific days for financial tasks.

Monthly money check-ins.

Automatic savings on payday.

Quarterly reviews.

Annual planning sessions.

Put them on a calendar.

Treat them like practice, not optional chores.

When something has a time and place, it gets done.

When it floats, it disappears.

Building a "Financial Practice Week"

Think in terms athletes understand.

What if your money had a practice week?

One day for reviewing accounts.

One day for budgeting adjustments.

One automated savings "rep."

One debt check-in.

One planning moment.

This does not need to take hours.

It needs to happen consistently.

Most financial progress happens in minutes, not marathons.

Ten minutes of review beats zero minutes of avoidance.

One automated transfer beats good intentions.

One scheduled check-in beats guessing.

Structure makes small actions powerful.

Accountability Without a Coach

After sports, accountability changes.

No one is checking your attendance.

No one is tracking your reps.

No one is enforcing standards.

That does not mean accountability disappears.

It means **you must design it**.

This might look like:

Using automation instead of memory.

Sharing goals with someone you trust.

Working with an advisor or coach.

Using reminders, checklists, or tools.

Tracking progress visually.

Athletes perform better when expectations are clear. Your financial life is no different.

If no one is watching, standards slip.

Build systems that watch for you.

Structure Creates Freedom, Not Restriction

Many people resist structure because they associate it with restriction.

Athletes know better.

Structure is what allowed you to perform freely.

It reduced chaos.

It protected energy.

It made execution automatic under pressure.

Financial structure does the same.

When money is organized, decisions get easier.

When savings are automated, stress decreases.

When bills are planned, surprises shrink.

When habits are consistent, confidence grows.

Structure is not about control.

It is about **capacity**.
Capacity to say yes.
Capacity to handle setbacks.
Capacity to plan long-term.

Coach's Perspective

A coach would recognize the problem immediately.
"You're not undisciplined.
You're unstructured."
And the solution would be familiar.
Create a plan.
Put it on the calendar.
Execute it consistently.
Adjust when needed.
Repeat.
No one expects perfection.
They expect effort within structure.

Game Situations and Decision Points

You notice you are reacting financially instead of planning.
Do you rebuild structure or keep improvising?
You miss savings for a few months.
Do you ignore it or reset the system?
You feel overwhelmed by money tasks.
Do you simplify the schedule or avoid it entirely?
Just like sports, the response determines the outcome.

Common Athlete Mistakes and Financial Parallels

Athletes rely on motivation.

Financially, that leads to inconsistency.

Athletes underestimate structure.

Financially, that leads to drift.

Athletes wait for pressure to act.

Financially, that leads to mistakes.

Structure prevents all three.

Winning the Long Game

Losing the schedule is one of the biggest hidden challenges former athletes face.

Rebuilding structure is one of the most powerful advantages you can create.

You already know how to follow systems.

You already know how to show up.

You already know how repetition creates results.

Apply that knowledge to your money.

Not through intensity.

Through structure.

That is how discipline survives when the whistle stops blowing.

Athlete Takeaways

Structure disappears quietly. Rebuild it intentionally.

Optional discipline is weaker than scheduled discipline.

Financial habits break when there is no calendar.

Replace practice schedules with personal systems.

Consistency comes from structure, not motivation.

Chapter 27: From Teammates to Coworkers

One of the strangest transitions after basketball has nothing to do with money on paper.

It is the people.

For most of your life, you lived in a locker room culture. Everyone knew why they were there. Everyone understood the goal. Roles were clear. Accountability was public. Feedback was constant. If you messed up, it showed on film. If you played well, it showed on film too.

Then you step into the workforce.

Suddenly, no one is watching film.

No one is explaining rotations.

No one is pulling you aside after every mistake.

And the people around you are not teammates. They are coworkers.

That shift feels subtle at first. Over time, it becomes one of the biggest reasons former athletes struggle with career progression, income growth, and long-term stability.

Why the Workplace Feels Foreign After Sports

Basketball environments are designed for clarity.

You know who the head coach is.

You know who sets the rotation.

You know who plays and who does not.

You know the scoreboard.

You know when you are winning and when you are not.

Most workplaces are not built that way.

Authority is spread out.

Feedback is inconsistent.

Expectations are rarely stated clearly.

Performance is often evaluated behind closed doors.

For former athletes, this creates confusion.

You are used to environments where effort is visible and results are measured openly. In the workplace, effort can be invisible and results can be subjective.

That does not mean the workplace is broken.

It means the rules are different.

Authority Without Coaches

In basketball, authority is obvious.

The coach sets the system.

Assistants reinforce it.

Veterans lead within it.

Everyone knows who has the final say.

In the workplace, authority is often unclear.

Your manager may not be the decision-maker.

Your boss may not control promotions.

Someone with no title may have influence.

Someone with a title may have none.

This is frustrating for athletes who are conditioned to respect hierarchy.

You want to know:

Who decides?

Who evaluates me?

Who do I listen to?

Who do I impress?

Without clarity, athletes often default to what worked before. They outwork everyone. They say yes to everything. They assume performance will be noticed.

Sometimes it is.

Often it is not.

Authority in the workplace is less visible and more political. That does not mean unethical. It means relational.

Learning who actually influences outcomes is a skill, not a flaw.

Feedback Without Film

Basketball gives constant feedback.

Film sessions.

Practice reps.

Stats.

Minutes played.

Coach conversations.

You always know where you stand.

In the workplace, feedback is rare and delayed.

You may not know you are struggling until review time.

You may not know you are doing well until someone else gets promoted.

You may not know expectations until you miss them.

This creates anxiety.

Former athletes are used to correcting mistakes quickly. Without feedback, you cannot adjust. You do not know if you are improving or falling behind.

The absence of feedback often leads athletes to overthink.

"Am I doing enough?"

"Am I missing something?"

"Why was that person promoted instead of me?"

This uncertainty affects confidence, performance, and decision-making.

It also impacts income.

When you do not understand how success is measured, negotiating raises, promotions, or new opportunities becomes harder.

Politics, Ambiguity, and Unclear Expectations

Basketball environments reward execution.

Workplace environments often reward perception.

This is one of the hardest truths for former athletes to accept.

You can execute perfectly and still lose opportunities if perception is misaligned. You can be average and advance quickly if perception is strong.

This feels unfair to athletes who grew up in merit-based systems.

But it is reality.

Politics does not mean manipulation.

It means relationships.

It means communication.

It means understanding how decisions are made.

Ambiguity exists because expectations are rarely written down clearly. Job descriptions describe tasks, not success. Performance metrics are often vague.

Athletes struggle here because they want clear roles.

"What does success look like?"

"What gets rewarded?"

"What gets ignored?"

If you do not ask these questions, you guess. Guessing leads to misalignment. Misalignment leads to stalled careers.

Why This Impacts Income Growth

Income growth is rarely automatic.

Raises are not guaranteed.

Promotions are not linear.

Effort alone is not enough.

Athletes often assume that if they work hard and stay loyal, income will follow. Sometimes it does. Often it does not.

Without understanding workplace dynamics, former athletes may:

Stay too long in roles that do not reward growth

Accept below-market pay because they undervalue negotiation

Avoid uncomfortable conversations about compensation

Miss opportunities because they do not advocate for themselves

Basketball teaches you to let your play speak.

The workplace often requires you to speak for your play.

This is uncomfortable for many athletes.

Career Stability Without a Team Structure

Teams provide built-in stability.

Your role may change, but the season continues.

You are protected by contracts, scholarships, or roster spots.

Your identity is tied to the team.

In the workforce, stability must be built.

Jobs change.

Managers leave.

Companies restructure.

Industries shift.

Former athletes often tie their identity to performance and loyalty. When workplaces change unexpectedly, it feels personal.

Career stability comes from skills, relationships, adaptability, and financial buffers.

Not from titles.

Not from tenure.

Not from effort alone.

Translating Team Skills to Workplace Success

The good news is that athletes are not disadvantaged.

They are just under-informed.

Athletes bring powerful skills into the workplace:

Discipline

Coachability

Work ethic

Resilience

Team awareness

Performance under pressure

The key is learning how to apply them in a different environment.

Instead of waiting for feedback, ask for it.

Instead of assuming effort is visible, communicate impact.

Instead of avoiding negotiation, prepare for it.

Instead of relying on loyalty, build optionality.

These are learnable skills.

Coach's Perspective

If a coach were watching this transition, they would recognize the issue immediately.

"You're still playing team basketball in a pickup game."

The advice would be familiar.

Learn the system.

Understand the roles.

Communicate.

Adjust.

Do not assume effort equals results.

The game is different, but the fundamentals still apply.

Game Situations and Decision Points

You feel undervalued at work.

Do you ask for clarity or stay silent?

You receive vague feedback.

Do you request specifics or guess?

You are offered a new role.

Do you evaluate growth potential or just title and pay?

You feel uncomfortable negotiating.

Do you avoid it or prepare like a game?

These moments shape careers the same way late-game decisions shape outcomes.

Common Athlete Mistakes and Financial Parallels

Athletes wait to be noticed.

Financially, that leads to stagnant income.

Athletes avoid difficult conversations.

Financially, that leads to underpayment.

Athletes assume loyalty is rewarded.

Financially, that leads to missed opportunities.

Awareness changes outcomes.

Winning the Long Game

Basketball prepared you to compete.

It did not prepare you to navigate ambiguity.

That does not make you behind.

It makes you early in a new learning curve.

The athletes who succeed long-term are the ones who adapt without losing their identity. They learn the new game without abandoning discipline, integrity, or effort.

They understand that coworkers are not teammates, but collaboration still matters.

They accept that feedback is not automatic and seek it intentionally.

They recognize that income growth requires communication, not just execution.

That is how careers stabilize.

That is how income grows.

That is how confidence returns.

Athlete Takeaways

The workplace feels foreign because the rules are different.

Authority is less visible. Learn where influence lives.

Feedback is rare. Ask for it instead of guessing.

Politics exist. Ignoring them does not protect you.

Income growth requires communication, not just effort.

Adapt your team skills to a new system and stay in the game.

Chapter 28: When No One Is Watching Anymore

Every basketball player remembers this moment.

The gym is empty.

No coach on the baseline.

No teammates watching.

No scoreboard.

No crowd.

Just you, the ball, and the decision of whether you are going to work.

This is where careers are made or quietly lost.

During your playing years, accountability was constant. Practice times were mandatory. Conditioning was enforced. Film exposed everything. Even on bad days, structure forced discipline. You showed up whether you felt like it or not.

Then basketball ends.

And suddenly, no one is watching anymore.

No one is checking if you reviewed your budget.

No one is tracking whether you saved this month.

No one is holding you accountable for long-term decisions.

No one is calling you out when you take shortcuts.

This is where many former athletes struggle. Not because they lack discipline, but because the system that enforced discipline disappears.

The Discipline Gap After Accountability Disappears

Basketball discipline is externally enforced.

You train because practice is scheduled.

You lift because it is required.

You watch film because it is expected.

You compete because your spot depends on it.

Adult life is different.

Discipline becomes optional.

You can skip saving this month.

You can avoid looking at your bank account.

You can ignore debt balances.

You can delay planning for years.

Nothing breaks immediately.

That is the danger.

The absence of consequences in the short term creates the illusion that everything is fine. But discipline does not disappear all at once. It erodes quietly.

This gap between external accountability and self-accountability is where most financial problems begin.

Why Former Athletes Self-Sabotage Without Pressure

This may be uncomfortable, but it is important.

Many former athletes do not fail financially because they are reckless.

They fail because they relax too much when the pressure is gone.

Pressure kept habits sharp.

Pressure forced preparation.

Pressure prevented drift.

Without it, comfort takes over.

Comfort sounds harmless.

Comfort feels earned.

Comfort feels deserved.

But comfort without structure leads to decay.

Skipping one savings contribution does not hurt.

Ignoring one credit card statement does not hurt.

Delaying one decision does not hurt.

Years later, the damage is obvious.

In basketball terms, this is losing edge in the offseason. You do not feel worse immediately. You feel it months later when conditioning is gone and timing is off.

Comfort vs Growth Decisions

Every day after sports presents a choice.

Comfort or growth.

Comfort is sleeping in.

Comfort is spending without thinking.

Comfort is avoiding hard conversations.

Comfort is telling yourself you will fix it later.

Growth is uncomfortable.

Growth is budgeting when no one is forcing you.

Growth is saving when it is easier to spend.

Growth is planning for a future you cannot yet see.

Growth is saying no when no one would blame you for saying yes.

Basketball taught you to choose growth when the reward was clear.

Adult life asks you to choose growth without immediate feedback.

That is harder.

The people who win financially are not the most aggressive or the most talented. They are the ones who consistently choose growth when comfort is available.

Translating "Grind Culture" Into Adult Life

Athletes are raised on grind culture.

Outwork everyone.

Be the first in.

Be the last out.

Sacrifice now.

Win later.

That mindset works in basketball.

Financially, it needs translation.

Grinding without direction leads to burnout.

Working harder without systems leads to frustration.

Earning more without structure leads to lifestyle inflation.

Adult discipline is not about grinding harder.

It is about building systems that work even when motivation fades.

Automation replaces willpower.

Rules replace emotion.

Structure replaces pressure.

Instead of grinding every day, you design a system that grinds for you.

Automatic savings.

Scheduled reviews.

Spending rules.

Decision frameworks.

That is mature discipline.

Why Money Mistakes Show Up Years Later

Most money mistakes do not explode immediately.

They show up slowly.

No emergency fund leads to debt years later.

Ignoring retirement leads to stress decades later.

Lifestyle creep leads to feeling trapped later.

Poor credit decisions limit options later.

This delayed impact is why athletes struggle.

Basketball consequences are immediate.

Money consequences are patient.

You do not feel the pain until the window to fix it cheaply has closed.

In basketball terms, this is ignoring fundamentals early in the season and paying for it in March when there is no time to correct it.

The mistake was not the final loss.

The mistake was the months of drift before it.

Discipline Without Applause

One of the hardest adjustments for former athletes is learning to perform without recognition.

No one applauds saving.

No one celebrates budgeting.

No one notices consistency.

No one cares that you avoided a bad decision.

But this is where financial independence is built.

You are training for a season no one sees.

You are preparing for moments no one will celebrate.

You are building options quietly.

That is adult discipline.

It looks boring.

It feels lonely.

It works.

Coach's Perspective

If a coach were watching your financial habits, the message would be familiar.

"No one is watching right now. That's why it matters."

Championship habits are built when no one is paying attention.

So are financial ones.

The coach would not yell.

They would not threaten.

They would remind you of who you are.

Discipline is who you are when accountability disappears.

Game Situations and Decision Points

You get paid and feel like treating yourself.

Do you follow the system or break it?

You have not reviewed your finances in months.

Do you avoid it or face it?

You feel comfortable and stable.

Do you assume it will last or prepare anyway?

These are not dramatic moments.

They are defining ones.

Common Athlete Mistakes and Financial Parallels

Athletes rely on external pressure.

Financially, that leads to drift when it disappears.

Athletes reward themselves too early.

Financially, that leads to lifestyle creep.

Athletes confuse rest with complacency.

Financially, that leads to stagnation.

Awareness changes behavior.

Winning the Long Game

Basketball ends.

Discipline does not have to.

The athletes who succeed long-term are not the ones who try to recreate the pressure of competition. They are the ones who replace it with structure.

They stop asking, “Do I feel like it?”

They start asking, "What does the system say?"

They understand that comfort is not the enemy.

Uncontrolled comfort is.

When no one is watching, you are still playing.

The scoreboard is just delayed.

Athlete Takeaways

Discipline becomes optional when accountability disappears.

Comfort slowly erodes habits if structure is not rebuilt.

Growth requires choosing discomfort without applause.

Grind culture must become system culture.

Money mistakes are delayed, not absent.

Who you are when no one is watching determines long-term success.

Chapter 29: Redefining Winning After the Uniform Comes Off

Every basketball player knows what winning looks like when the uniform is on.

The scoreboard tells you.

The stats confirm it.

The film backs it up.

Points.

Minutes.

Wins.

Playing time.

Championships.

Success is visible, measurable, and agreed upon by everyone in the gym.

Then the uniform comes off.

And suddenly, the scoreboard disappears.

No box score.

No standings.

No rankings.

No clear definition of who is winning and who is not.

That is where many former athletes get lost.

Not because they stop competing.

But because they start competing on the wrong scoreboard.

Why Chasing Status Replaces Chasing Performance

When structure disappears, people look for substitutes.

After sports, performance becomes harder to measure. Progress is slower. Feedback is inconsistent. Recognition is rare. That vacuum creates discomfort.

So the brain looks for something familiar.

Status.

Income.

Titles.

Cars.

Houses.

Job labels.

Visible markers that say, "I'm doing well."

Status feels like winning because it looks like winning.

But status is not the same as performance.

In basketball terms, this is confusing points with impact. A player can score and still hurt the team. A player can sacrifice stats and elevate everyone else.

After sports, many athletes chase what looks impressive instead of what actually works long term.

Status is loud.

Performance is quiet.

Income vs Fulfillment

Income matters.

It pays bills.

It creates options.

It reduces stress.

But income alone is not fulfillment.

Many former athletes hit income milestones they once dreamed about and still feel unsettled. Something feels off. Motivation drops. Satisfaction fades. The question becomes uncomfortable:

"If this is winning, why does it not feel like it?"

In basketball terms, this is making the league but losing the love of the game. You achieved the goal, but the experience does not match the expectation.

Fulfillment comes from alignment.

Do your values match how you spend your time?

Does your work use your strengths?

Does your life feel intentional or reactive?

Income supports fulfillment.

It does not replace it.

Athletes who confuse the two often keep chasing more money, assuming fulfillment will show up later. Sometimes it does not.

Titles, Houses, Cars, and Comparison Traps

Comparison never leaves athletics.

It just changes uniforms.

After sports, the comparison traps look like this:

Who makes more?

Who got promoted faster?

Who bought the bigger house?

Who drives the nicer car?

Who looks more successful online?

These comparisons are dangerous because they ignore context.

You do not see:

Debt.

Stress.

Lack of flexibility.

Unfulfilling work.

Strained relationships.

Burnout.

In basketball terms, this is comparing stat lines without watching the game film. You miss the defensive breakdowns. You miss the missed rotations. You miss the full picture.

Comparison distorts decision-making.

It pushes people to:

Spend too much.

Take jobs they hate.

Delay balance.

Ignore warning signs.

Comparison replaces intention with reaction.

Why Athletes Feel Pressure to "Look Successful"

Athletes are used to visibility.

People watched you play.

They knew your role.

They knew when you were winning.

After sports, invisibility feels uncomfortable.

So many former athletes feel pressure to prove they are still relevant. Still winning. Still impressive.

That pressure shows up financially.

Lifestyle inflation.

Overspending.

Chasing optics.

Avoiding humility.

In basketball terms, this is forcing shots to prove you belong instead of letting the game come to you.

The need to look successful often leads people away from becoming successful.

What "Success" Actually Looks Like in Your 30s and 40s

This is where the definition of winning needs to change.

Winning in your 30s and 40s is not louder.

It is steadier.

It looks like:

Control over your time.

Flexibility in your schedule.

Work that aligns with your strengths.

Savings that create options.

Health that supports longevity.

Relationships that are not sacrificed for optics.

Less stress, not more stuff.

In basketball terms, this is veteran basketball.

You may not jump as high.

You may not play as fast.

But the game slows down.

Decisions improve.

Efficiency increases.

Winning becomes about sustainability, not highlights.

Building a New Scoreboard

After sports, you need a new way to measure progress.

If you do not define it, society will define it for you.

And society usually defines success by status.

A healthy scoreboard might include:

How much margin do I have?

How flexible is my life?

How often do I feel rushed?

Am I building or just maintaining?

Do my choices reflect my values?

Am I progressing or just staying busy?

These metrics do not trend on social media.

They do not show up on résumés.

They do not impress strangers.

They matter more.

In basketball terms, this is internal accountability. You know when you played well even if no one noticed.

Letting Go of the Old Scoreboard

This is hard.

Athletes are wired to compete.

To measure.

To rank.

To win.

Letting go of the old scoreboard can feel like giving up.

It is not.

It is leveling up.

You are not quitting competition.

You are choosing a longer game.

The athlete who keeps chasing status often burns out.

The athlete who redefines winning builds something that lasts.

Coach's Perspective

If a coach were guiding you through this transition, the message would be familiar.

"Stop playing someone else's game."

You do not measure success by someone else's role.

You do not judge progress by someone else's timeline.

You do not force plays that do not fit your system.

Great teams play to their identity.

Great lives do the same.

Game Situations and Decision Points

You are offered a higher-paying role that costs you flexibility.

Do you take it automatically or evaluate the trade-off?

You feel behind because of comparison.

Do you react emotionally or revisit your scoreboard?

You achieve a goal but still feel empty.

Do you chase another milestone or reassess alignment?

These are not financial decisions.

They are identity decisions.

Common Athlete Mistakes and Financial Parallels

Athletes chase status instead of impact.

Financially, that leads to misaligned lives.

Athletes compare without context.

Financially, that leads to poor decisions.

Athletes confuse activity with progress.

Financially, that leads to burnout.

Awareness breaks the cycle.

Winning the Long Game

The uniform comes off.

The crowd fades.

The noise quiets.

What remains is how you live.

Winning after sports is not about being impressive.

It is about being intentional.

It is about building a life that supports who you are now, not who you were at 22.

You do not need a louder scoreboard.

You need the right one.

Athlete Takeaways

Status is not the same as performance.

Income supports fulfillment but does not replace it.

Comparison distorts judgment and accelerates bad decisions.

Success in your 30s and 40s is about stability, flexibility, and alignment.

You must build a new scoreboard or inherit the wrong one.

Winning long-term requires redefining what winning means.

Chapter 30: Staying Connected Without Living in the Past

Every basketball player remembers the locker room.

The jokes.

The routines.

The shared exhaustion.

The unspoken understanding that everyone in that room was pulling in the same direction.

That environment is rare.

When the season ends and the uniform comes off, most athletes do not realize what they are actually losing. It is not just the game. It is the built-in community. The daily interaction. The shared purpose. The sense of belonging that required no explanation.

After sports, that disappears almost overnight.

And if it is not replaced intentionally, isolation fills the gap.

The Role of Community After Sports

Basketball is not an individual sport, even when one player has the ball.

Every possession depends on spacing, communication, trust, and timing. The game teaches you, without ever saying it directly, that progress happens in groups.

After sports, many former athletes try to operate solo.

They assume independence means doing everything alone. Handling problems quietly. Not asking for help. Not needing anyone.

That mindset creates distance.

Community is not weakness.

It is infrastructure.

The most successful former athletes rebuild community deliberately. Not by recreating the past, but by building new locker rooms that fit the next phase of life.

Why Isolation Hits Former Athletes Hard

Isolation feels heavier for athletes because the contrast is so extreme.

You go from:

Daily interaction

Constant feedback

Shared goals

High accountability

To:

Working alone

Ambiguous expectations

Delayed feedback

Independent decision-making

The drop-off is sudden.

In basketball terms, it is like going from a full-court game to shooting alone in an empty gym. The reps still count, but the energy is different. Motivation changes. Accountability fades.

Isolation often shows up quietly.

Less structure.

Less urgency.

Less joy.

More comparison.

More self-doubt.

Without community, discipline erodes. And when discipline erodes, financial and personal mistakes show up faster.

Mentorship: Replacing Coaches Without Replacing Authority

Every athlete understands the value of a good coach.

Someone who has been there.

Someone who sees what you miss.

Someone who challenges you without tearing you down.

After sports, many athletes resist mentorship because it feels like going backward. Like admitting you do not know something.

That resistance costs years.

Mentorship after sports is not about hierarchy.

It is about perspective.

A mentor helps you:

Avoid mistakes you do not see coming

Reframe setbacks

Understand systems outside athletics

Translate discipline into a new environment

In basketball terms, this is film study with someone who understands the game at a different level.

You still make the plays.

They help you see the floor.

Finding Purpose Without the Team

This is one of the hardest transitions.

In sports, purpose is assigned.

Practice today.

Game tomorrow.

Win this week.

Advance next round.

After sports, purpose must be chosen.

That feels uncomfortable at first.

Without a team, many former athletes drift. They stay busy but feel unfulfilled. They work hard but lack direction. They confuse motion with meaning.

Purpose after sports is not about replacing basketball.

It is about redirecting the qualities basketball built.

Competition becomes excellence.

Teamwork becomes leadership.

Discipline becomes consistency.

Preparation becomes planning.

Resilience becomes adaptability.

In basketball terms, this is learning to impact the game without scoring.

Purpose evolves.

It is not handed to you anymore.

Healthy Nostalgia vs Being Stuck

Missing the game is normal.

Missing the locker room.

Missing the routine.

Missing the clarity.

Nostalgia becomes unhealthy when it turns into comparison.

"When I played, things made sense."

"I peaked back then."

"Nothing will feel like that again."

Those thoughts freeze growth.

Healthy nostalgia honors the past.

Unhealthy nostalgia anchors you to it.

In basketball terms, this is watching old highlights instead of studying current film. It feels good, but it does not help you improve today.

The goal is not to forget the past.

The goal is to integrate it.

Your identity is bigger than one chapter.

Creating New Locker Rooms

New locker rooms do not look like old ones.

They might be:

Professional communities

Entrepreneur groups

Faith-based groups

Former athlete networks

Mentorship circles

Volunteer teams

Training partners

Family units

The common thread is shared direction.

A locker room is not about proximity.

It is about alignment.

Strong locker rooms provide:

Accountability

Perspective

Support

Shared standards

Belonging without performance pressure

You do not need many.

You need the right ones.

Identity After Basketball

The hardest shift is internal.

For years, you were introduced as an athlete.

Known as a player.

Defined by performance.

After sports, that label fades.

If you do not replace it intentionally, you cling to it.

Identity after basketball should be built forward, not backward.

You are not a former athlete.
You are an athlete in a new arena.
The traits that made you successful did not disappear.
They need a new outlet.

Coach's Perspective

If a coach were guiding you through this phase, the message would be steady.
"Do not isolate."
"Find your people."
"Stay accountable."
"Keep growing."
No coach sends a player onto the court alone.
No one builds a life alone either.

Game Situations and Decision Points

You feel disconnected.
Do you withdraw or reach out?
You miss the team.
Do you relive the past or build something new?
You feel lost.
Do you wait for clarity or create structure?
Connection is a choice.
So is growth.

Common Athlete Mistakes and Financial Parallels

Athletes isolate instead of adapting.
Financially, that leads to blind spots.
Athletes cling to past identity.
Financially, that leads to stagnation.
Athletes avoid new locker rooms.

Financially, that leads to missed opportunity.

The same discipline that built success in basketball builds connection after it.

Winning the Long Game

Basketball ends.

Community should not.

The athletes who thrive after sports are not the ones who move on the fastest or forget the game entirely. They are the ones who carry the lessons forward while building something new.

Connection fuels discipline.

Discipline fuels consistency.

Consistency fuels long-term success.

You do not need to live in the past to honor it.

You need to stay connected while moving forward.

Athlete Takeaways

Community matters as much after sports as it did during them.

Isolation hits former athletes harder because the contrast is extreme.

Mentorship replaces coaches with perspective, not control.

Purpose must be chosen, not assigned.

Healthy nostalgia honors the past without anchoring you to it.

New locker rooms create accountability and belonging.

Your identity should move forward, not stay frozen in time.

The uniform comes off.

The lessons stay.

The next chapter is yours to build.

Glossary of Wrestling and Financial Terms

This glossary connects key financial concepts to familiar ideas from **wrestling**, making money easier to understand through the language, structure, discipline, and repetition wrestlers already know.

Asset Allocation

Financial Definition:

How money is divided among different investment types such as stocks, bonds, and cash to balance risk and return.

Wrestling Comparison:

How training time, energy, and match strategy are distributed across strength, conditioning, technique, and recovery. Overemphasizing one area without balance leads to breakdowns under pressure.

Assets

Financial Definition:

Things you own that have value, such as cash, investments, real estate, or retirement accounts.

Wrestling Comparison:

Your strengths as a wrestler. Technique, conditioning, mat awareness, experience, and preparation that contribute to consistent performance.

Bonds

Financial Definition:

Loans made to governments or companies that pay interest and return principal over time.

Wrestling Comparison:

Base position and control. Not flashy, but essential for stability when matches get tight and fatigue sets in.

Budget

Financial Definition:

A plan for how income is allocated toward expenses, savings, and goals.

Wrestling Comparison:

Match pacing and energy management. If you do not control tempo and positioning, execution breaks down late.

Cash Flow

Financial Definition:

Money coming in versus money going out.

Wrestling Comparison:

Gas tank management. If you expend too much energy early, you struggle to finish strong.

Compounding

Financial Definition:

Earnings that generate additional earnings over time.

Wrestling Comparison:

Daily drilling and muscle memory. Each rep builds on the last and makes execution more automatic over time.

Credit

Financial Definition:

The ability to borrow money with the promise of repayment.

Wrestling Comparison:

Trust with referees and coaches. When earned and managed well, it gives freedom. When abused, it creates limitations.

Debt

Financial Definition:

Money borrowed that must be repaid, often with interest.

Wrestling Comparison:

Extra weight or fatigue. Manageable in small amounts, dangerous when excessive and poorly controlled.

Diversification

Financial Definition:

Spreading investments across different assets to reduce risk.

Wrestling Comparison:

Not relying on one move or one style to win every match. Versatility keeps you competitive.

Emergency Fund

Financial Definition:

Savings set aside for unexpected expenses.

Wrestling Comparison:

Conditioning buffer. You hope you never need it, but it prevents collapse when things go wrong.

ETF (Exchange-Traded Fund)

Financial Definition:

A fund that holds many investments and trades like a stock.

Wrestling Comparison:

A full training room instead of solo workouts. Team systems reduce individual mistakes.

Fees / Expense Ratios

Financial Definition:

Costs associated with managing investments.

Wrestling Comparison:

Poor positioning or wasted motion. Small inefficiencies that quietly drain stamina over time.

Growth Investing

Financial Definition:

Investing in companies expected to grow faster than average.

Wrestling Comparison:

High-risk attacks and aggressive offense. Higher upside, but only effective with strong fundamentals.

Insurance

Financial Definition:

Protection against financial loss from unexpected events.

Wrestling Comparison:

Protective gear and injury prevention. You do not compete without protection when risk is present.

Liquidity

Financial Definition:

How easily money can be accessed without penalty or delay.

Wrestling Comparison:

Ability to scramble and adjust when a position breaks down. Flexibility keeps you alive in tough moments.

Net Worth

Financial Definition:

Assets minus liabilities.

Wrestling Comparison:

Overall match control. Not one takedown, but the full six minutes.

Rebalancing

Financial Definition:

Adjusting investments back to their intended mix over time.

Wrestling Comparison:

Mid-match adjustments when an opponent changes tactics.

Risk

Financial Definition:

The chance that outcomes differ from expectations, including loss.

Wrestling Comparison:

Move selection. Higher reward techniques carry higher risk if timing or position is off.

Roth IRA

Financial Definition:

A retirement account where money grows tax-free if rules are followed.

Wrestling Comparison:

Front-loaded conditioning. Harder early work that makes later rounds easier.

Stocks

Financial Definition:

Ownership shares in a company.

Wrestling Comparison:

Primary offensive attacks. They drive scoring but require setup and control.

Tax-Advantaged Accounts

Financial Definition:

Accounts that provide tax benefits, often with rules and restrictions.

Wrestling Comparison:

Structured training programs. Rules exist to improve long-term outcomes.

Volatility

Financial Definition:

Short-term ups and downs in market value.

Wrestling Comparison:

A brief scramble. Normal movement that only becomes dangerous if you panic.

Permanent Loss

Financial Definition:

Money that cannot recover due to poor decisions or panic.

Wrestling Comparison:

Being pinned. Usually the result of abandoning fundamentals.

Total Return

Financial Definition:

Investment return from both price growth and income.

Wrestling Comparison:

The final score plus match control. Every point matters.

Value Investing

Financial Definition:

Investing in assets believed to be undervalued.

Wrestling Comparison:

Solid fundamentals and positional dominance. Less flash, more control.

Yield

Financial Definition:

Income generated from an investment.

Wrestling Comparison:

Consistent scoring. Not dramatic, but reliable.

Final Note

This glossary reinforces one core principle:

Financial success, like success in **wrestling**, comes from balance, discipline, timing, and repetition.

That philosophy runs through **WrestlingMoney101** and extends far beyond the mat.

Disclaimers

WrestlingMoney101

This book is for educational purposes only.

The information provided in **WrestlingMoney101** is intended to help readers understand general financial concepts using wrestling-based analogies. It is **not** individualized financial, investment, tax, legal, or insurance advice.

Every financial situation is different. Your goals, income, family circumstances, risk tolerance, and time horizon are unique. What works for one person may not be appropriate for another.

Not Financial, Investment, or Legal Advice

Nothing in this book should be interpreted as a recommendation to buy, sell, or hold any specific investment, financial product, or strategy.

This book does not replace advice from qualified professionals such as:

- Financial advisors
- Accountants or tax professionals
- Attorneys
- Insurance professionals

Before making financial decisions, readers should consult professionals who can evaluate their individual situation.

No Guarantees or Promises of Results

All investing involves risk, including the possible loss of principal.

Past performance does not guarantee future results. Markets fluctuate. Economic conditions change. Outcomes cannot be predicted or guaranteed.

The examples and scenarios in this book are illustrative only and may not reflect actual results or real-world outcomes.

Tax and Legal Information

Any discussion of taxes, retirement accounts, estate planning, or legal structures is general in nature.

Tax laws and regulations change frequently and vary by jurisdiction. Legal requirements differ based on location and personal circumstances.

Readers should seek personalized tax or legal advice before acting on any information related to these topics.

Athlete and Career Considerations

This book discusses financial topics as they relate to athletes and former athletes, including career transitions, variable income, and post-competition financial realities.

It does **not** provide career placement services, employment advice, or guarantees related to income, compensation, or career success.

Use of Analogies

Wrestling and sports analogies are used to make financial concepts easier to understand.

These analogies are educational tools only and should not be interpreted literally. Financial decisions require analysis beyond analogy.

Personal Responsibility

By reading this book, you acknowledge that:

- You are responsible for your own financial decisions
- You understand that financial outcomes involve uncertainty
- You agree to seek appropriate professional guidance when needed

Education improves decision-making, but responsibility remains with the individual.

Contact Information

If you would like to learn more about the concepts discussed in this book or explore additional educational resources, **Pat Brown** can be found through public platforms including LinkedIn, Twitter, and via Google search.

For questions specifically related to **WrestlingMoney101**, you may contact Pat Brown at:

info@wrestlingmoney101.com

(or replace with the appropriate series email address)

Final Reminder

Financial success is built over time through discipline, planning, and consistency.

This book provides a framework, not a guarantee.

Use it as a guide, not a substitute for professional advice.

Pat Brown OLB, University of Kansas

Made in the USA
Monee, IL
04 November 2026

67387613R00148